THE COMPLETE IDIOT'S GUIDE® TO

Facebook

Third Edition

by Mikal E. Belicove and Joe Kraynak

ALPHA

A member of Penguin Group (USA) Inc.

ALPHA BOOKS

Published by Penguin Group (USA) Inc.

Penguin Group (USA) Inc., 375 Hudson Street, New York, New York 10014, USA • Penguin Group (Canada), 90 Eglinton Avenue East, Suite 700, Toronto, Ontario M4P 2Y3, Canada (a division of Pearson Penguin Canada Inc.) • Penguin Books Ltd., 80 Strand, London WC2R 0RL, England • Penguin Ireland, 25 St. Stephen's Green, Dublin 2, Ireland (a division of Penguin Books Ltd.) • Penguin Group (Australia), 250 Camberwell Road, Camberwell, Victoria 3124, Australia (a division of Pearson Australia Group Pty. Ltd.) • Penguin Books India Pvt. Ltd., 11 Community Centre, Panchsheel Park, New Delhi—110 017, India • Penguin Group (NZ), 67 Apollo Drive, Rosedale, North Shore, Auckland 1311, New Zealand (a division of Pearson New Zealand Ltd.) • Penguin Books (South Africa) (Pty.) Ltd., 24 Sturdee Avenue, Rosebank, Johannesburg 2196, South Africa • Penguin Books Ltd., Registered Offices: 80 Strand, London WC2R 0RL, England

International Standard Book Number: 978-1-61564-216-8
Library of Congress Catalog Card Number: 2012935354

14 13 12   8 7 6 5 4 3 2 1

Interpretation of the printing code: The rightmost number of the first series of numbers is the year of the book's printing; the rightmost number of the second series of numbers is the number of the book's printing. For example, a printing code of 12-1 shows that the first printing occurred in 2012.

Printed in the United States of America

Note: This publication contains the opinions and ideas of its authors. It is intended to provide helpful and informative material on the subject matter covered. It is sold with the understanding that the authors and publisher are not engaged in rendering professional services in the book. If the reader requires personal assistance or advice, a competent professional should be consulted.

The authors and publisher specifically disclaim any responsibility for any liability, loss, or risk, personal or otherwise, which is incurred as a consequence, directly or indirectly, of the use and application of any of the contents of this book.

Most Alpha books are available at special quantity discounts for bulk purchases for sales promotions, premiums, fund-raising, or educational use. Special books, or book excerpts, can also be created to fit specific needs.

For details, write: Special Markets, Alpha Books, 375 Hudson Street, New York, NY 10014.

Publisher: *Mike Sanders*

Executive Managing Editor: *Billy Fields*

Senior Acquisitions Editor: *Tom Stevens*

Development Editor: *Ginny Bess Munroe*

Senior Production Editor: *Janette Lynn*

Copy Editor: *Jan Zoya*

Cover Designer: *Kurt Owens*

Book Designers: *William Thomas, Rebecca Batchelor*

Indexer: *Johnna Vahoose Dinse*

Layout: *Ayanna Lacey*

Proofreader: *John Etchison*

From Mikal: *To my 77-year-old mother, Glenda M. Belicove, who taught me everything I ever needed to know about living an authentic life, as well as a thing or two about using Facebook!*

From Joe: *To Facebook users worldwide who make Facebook the most intriguing digital hangout on the planet.*

Contents

Introduction

In the days B.C. (Before Computers), losing touch with friends and family was a part of life. You'd graduate and all your school chums would wander off in different directions. You'd leave your job and lose valuable contacts. Aunts, uncles, and cousins would fade into memories. Even keeping in touch with siblings hundreds or thousands of miles away was a challenge.

Facebook, with the help of computers and the internet, has reversed that trend. Not only does the world's largest and most popular social utility enable you to stay in touch with people, but it also facilitates the process of tracking down people you lost touch with years or decades ago. Facebook also provides numerous ways for you to engage and interact with all these folks daily—by sharing status updates, photos, and videos; posting links to favorite web pages or blogs; chatting; messaging; playing games; planning events; gathering in groups; and so on. And if you're running a business or organization (big or small), Facebook provides several valuable tools to keep in touch with customers, clients, and members right where many of them like to hang out most.

Perhaps best of all, Facebook is free, and all you need to get started is a computer with an internet connection and a desire to connect with others. If you're concerned about privacy, you'll be relieved to know that Facebook gives you complete control over whom you choose to "friend" and the information you choose to share.

If you're concerned that you don't know where to start, that's where we come in. In this book, we provide everything you need to know to get started on Facebook; track down friends, family members, colleagues, former classmates, and others; promote your business or organization or yourself; and tap the full potential of Facebook.

Disclaimer: Facebook is in a constant state of change as its developers introduce new features and adjust the ways that Facebook members interact with the service and with one another. During the writing of the book, we checked everything, step by step, not once, but twice to verify its accuracy prior to publication, but we're 99.99 percent sure that by the time you read this, something will have changed. We tried to make the instructions specific enough to be useful and general enough to cover minor changes, but you may need to consult Facebook's Help system for details and changes. We show you how in Chapter 1.

What You Learn in This Book

You don't have to read this book from cover to cover (although you might miss some succulent tidbits if you skip around). If you haven't even signed up with Facebook, start with Chapter 1 to register, log in, and take a brief tour of Facebook's core features. If you're concerned about privacy issues, skip to Chapter 2, where we show you how to adjust your privacy settings. To track down people and invite them to be your Facebook friends, head to Chapter 4. Chapter 7 shows you how to share photos, one of Facebook's most popular features.

As for the rest of the chapters, each covers a specific Facebook feature. To provide some structure for this hodgepodge of features, we've grouped the chapters into the following four parts and tacked on a glossary at the end:

Part 1, Mastering Facebook Basics, shows you how to sign up, sign in, add a photo and information to your Facebook Profile, tweak the privacy settings to your comfort level, track down friends and family and add them as Facebook friends, keep in touch with friends via Timelines and News Feeds, and contact people in private via the Message feature (email, chat, and voice/video conferencing). We also show you how to leave Facebook with or without leaving personal information behind.

Part 2, Getting More Involved with Facebook, ramps you up to some more advanced Facebook features, including photo sharing, video sharing, groups, and events. For parents, teachers, and others responsible for the safety of children and adolescents, we've included a chapter on Facebook safety. After logging on and figuring out what the Timeline and News Feed are all about, these are the features you tackle next.

Part 3, Harnessing the Power of Facebook Apps, introduces you to some higher-level applications (or apps, for short) designed to enhance the Facebook experience. Here, you learn how to access core Facebook apps, explore Facebook's robust collection of third-party apps, and use the Mobile app to access Facebook from your smartphone.

Part 4, Utilizing Facebook for Businesses and Organizations, helps you unleash the power of social-media marketing on Facebook. After a brief chapter on how you can use Facebook to promote yourself, your business or organization, or your products and services, we show you how to create and promote a Facebook page (sometimes called a fan page); use Facebook ads to drive traffic to your website, blog, or page; and strengthen your brand.

Conventions Used in This Book

We use several conventions in this book to make it easier to understand. For example, when you need to type something, it appears **bold**.

Likewise, if we tell you to select or click a command, the command appears **bold**. This enables you to quickly scan a series of steps without having to wade through all the text.

Extras

A plethora of sidebars offer additional information about what you've just read. Here's what to look for:

FRIEND-LY ADVICE

During our days on Facebook, we discovered easier, faster, and better ways to perform certain tasks and maximize the power of specific features. Here, we share these tips with you.

WHOA!

Before you click that button, skim the page for one of these sidebars, each of which offers a precautionary note. Chances are, we've made the mistake ourselves, so let us tell you how to avoid the same blunder.

> **POKE**
>
> On Facebook, you can poke your Facebook friends when they're online to let them know you're thinking about them. As you might imagine, this can get annoying if someone overdoes it. We include pokes throughout the book to cue you in on lesser-known features of Facebook. Hopefully, you'll find our pokes more compelling than most.

Acknowledgments

Several people contributed to building and perfecting this book. We owe special thanks to Tom Stevens for choosing us to author this book and for handling the assorted details to get it in gear. Thanks to Ginny Munroe for guiding the content, keeping it focused on new users, ferreting out all our typos, and fine-tuning our sentences. Jan Lynn deserves a free trip to Paris for shepherding the manuscript (and art) through production. The Alpha Books production team merits a round of applause for transforming a collection of electronic files into such an attractive book.

Finally, we'd be remiss if we failed to thank the dozen or so Facebook members—our friends, both on and off Facebook—who served as guinea pigs and allowed us to capture their Facebook activity in the screen shots you see throughout this book. To Adam W. Chase, Al Rotches, Amy McCloskey Tobin, Andy Marker, BlackPast.org, Brighton Feed & Saddlery, Chris Ochs, Debra Oakland, Ford Reese Church, Glenda Belicove, Homemade harvey, Jay Muntz, Jennifer St. James, Jerry Chrisman, Michael McKenzie, Nirvana Grille, Paul Ford, Peter Leibfred, R. Scott Torgan, Sam Williams, Scott D. Slater, Stuart Lisonbee, Susan Cherones, and Tanya Payne, thank you very much; this book wouldn't have been possible without your witty status updates, photos, and more.

Trademarks

All terms mentioned in this book that are known to be or are suspected of being trademarks or service marks have been appropriately capitalized. Alpha Books and Penguin Group (USA) Inc. cannot attest to the accuracy of this information. Use of a term in this book should not be regarded as affecting the validity of any trademark or service mark.

Mastering Facebook Basics

Everyone on Facebook has had a first encounter with it—staring at the screen, bewildered as to what's going on, and uncertain on how to proceed. It's sort of like stepping foot in a foreign country, where you're unsure of the customs and can't even figure out how to plug in your hair dryer without turning it into toast.

In this part, we re-create the first-encounter experience without the fear and bewilderment. We show you how to sign up, sign in, flesh out your Profile, upload a Profile photo, protect your personal information, find people, make friends, and interact with others via Timelines and News Feeds. In other words, we bring you up to speed on the basics.

Meeting Facebook Face to Face

In This Chapter

- Finding out what this Facebook thing is all about
- Getting your face on Facebook
- Making your way around
- Brushing up on Facebook etiquette
- Getting help

Everyone seems to be on Facebook … except you. Well, that's about to change. It's high time to lose your Facebook virginity and join the rest of your friends and family in the twenty-first century. In this chapter, we introduce you to Facebook, show you how to register and log in, and then take you on a nickel tour to get you up to speed on the basics.

What Is Facebook, Anyway?

Facebook is a free online social-networking venue where friends, family, colleagues, and acquaintances can mingle, get to know one another better, and expand their social circles.

After you register and log in to Facebook, as explained in the following section, you can invite people you know to become your Facebook *friends*. You can even invite people who aren't Facebook members to join Facebook and become your friend, assuming you have the person's email address. Anyone you already know on

Facebook can invite you to become his or her Facebook friend, too. (We cover the whole making-friends thing in Chapter 4.)

Once you have a Facebook friend or two, you can begin sharing with them by posting status updates to your News Feed or Timeline. We've introduced a lot of Facebook terminology already, so let's define a few key terms:

- **Status update:** A brief message that tells your Facebook friends what you're doing, thinking, or feeling. A status update includes text, a photo, video clip, link to a website, or a question.

- **News Feed:** A running record of status updates and more posted by you and your friends.

- **Timeline:** An online scrapbook that documents your life on and off Facebook with content you choose to add to it or that you allow others to add, from your date of birth to the day you read this bullet. Everyone on Facebook has a Timeline he or she can customize. (Longtime Facebook users who haven't upgraded to the Timeline have a *Wall* instead, which functions as a more private place where a Facebook member and his or her friends can share content with one another.)

- **Ticker:** Real-time streaming status updates and news. You can also use the ticker to listen to music with friends or join in conversations over stories that appear in the ticker.

News Feed

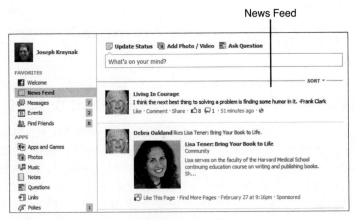

Your News Feed keeps you in touch with your friends.

That's Facebook in a nutshell, but you can do much more than simply swap updates with your buddies. Following are some of the more popular activities you might want to engage in:

- Dig up old friends and classmates.
- Track down family members who've wandered from the fold.
- Expand your social and professional circles by connecting with friends of friends and current and former co-workers.
- Share photos, videos, and links to interesting web pages.
- Recommend books, movies, and music.
- Exchange birthday wishes and gifts.
- Play games.
- Spread the word about political causes and charities.
- Invite guests to parties and other get-togethers and keep track of who's planning to attend.
- Text and audio/video chat with your friends online for free wherever they might be … assuming they're online when you are.
- Buy and sell stuff, find a job, and market yourself or your business.
- Build and grow a community around shared interests or beliefs.

POKE

Facebook is in a perpetual process of evolution. By the time you read this, additional features might be available.

Putting Your Face on Facebook

Before you can join the revelry, you have to put your face (and name) on Facebook by registering. This entails entering your email address, choosing a password, and providing some basic information about yourself, including your name, sex, and birthday. To register, follow these steps:

1. Fire up your web browser and head to www.facebook.com.

2. Complete the Sign Up form. It provides the instruction you need.

3. Click **Sign Up**. Facebook might display a security check screen prompting you to type a string of characters shown on the screen.

4. If a security check appears, type the text that appears as directed and click **Sign Up**.

5. Check the email for the address you used to sign up for Facebook, open the Facebook confirmation message, and click the link to confirm.

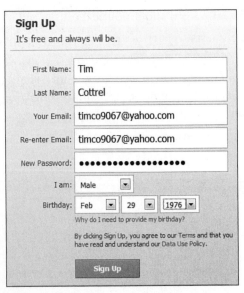

Complete the form and click **Sign Up**.

Finding Friends and Entering Your Info

After you register, Facebook steps you through the process of finding friends, entering basic information like schools you've attended and places you've worked, and uploading a digital photo of yourself. All of these steps are optional, so you can safely click **Skip this step** at each step and do all this later at your leisure. If you'd rather do it now, proceed to the following section.

Finding Friends Using Your Email Address Book

The first order of business is to find some friends. If the email address you used to sign on to Facebook is web-based, like Gmail (Google email), and your email account has an address book with contacts listed in it, Facebook can extract email addresses from your address book and use them to locate any Facebook members who log in using any of those addresses.

Don't worry, Facebook won't send out friend invitations to everyone in your address book without your permission. You'll have a chance to select the people you want to invite. To find potential friends now, enter the password associated with your email account, click **Find Friends**, and follow instructions. If you don't know your email password, you will be unable to use this feature. Try contacting your email service provider to have your password reset. For more about finding friends, see Chapter 4.

Facebook can find friends for you.

Entering School and Workplace Information

In Step 2 you're asked to enter information about your high school, college, and one place you've worked. Facebook uses this information to search for even more people you might know—people who graduated from the same high school or college the same year you did or who worked at the same company.

Enter any or all of the requested information and click **Save & Continue** or just click **Skip this step**.

Enter school and workplace information to enlist Facebook's assistance in tracking down classmates and co-workers.

If you choose **Save & Continue**, Facebook displays a selection of Facebook members it has identified as people with whom you might have graduated or worked. Click **Add as friend** next to each person you want to request to be a friend and click **Save & Continue**, or click **Skip** to skip this step.

Facebook displays the third step in getting started: uploading a photo of yourself, as discussed next.

Uploading a Digital Photo of Yourself

If you have a digital photo of yourself stored on your computer, or a webcam plugged into your computer so you can take a photo of yourself, you can add your mug shot, called a *Profile picture*, to your Profile. In Step 3 of getting started, click **Upload a Photo** or **Take a Photo**.

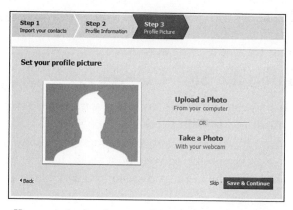

You can upload a photo or take a photo using a webcam.

If you click **Upload a Photo**, the Upload Your Profile Picture dialog box appears, prompting you to specify the photo file you want to use. Click **Browse**, use the resulting dialog box to select a digital photo of yourself stored on your computer, and click **Open**. Facebook uploads the photo and inserts it in your Profile.

If you click **Take a Photo**, the Take a Photo dialog box appears. If the Adobe Flash Player Settings dialog box appears, click **Allow** and then **Close**. Click the camera icon, say "Cheese" into your webcam, and wait three seconds for Facebook to snap your photo. If you like what you see, click **Save Picture**. If you don't like it, click **Cancel** and reshoot.

You can snap a picture of yourself using a webcam.

When you're happy with your Profile picture, click **Save & Continue**.

Completing the Sign-Up Process

Facebook logs you in and displays a screen with additional steps you can take at this time, including any steps you skipped during the sign-up process. It's a good idea to go through these steps now so Facebook doesn't keep bugging you about them, but you can skip them by clicking **Home** in the top menu (the dark blue bar).

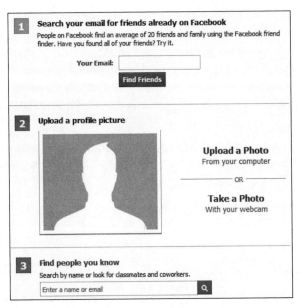

Facebook gives you an opportunity to complete steps you skipped.

Logging In and Logging Out

Now that you have a username (your email address) and password, you can log in and out of Facebook whenever the spirit moves you. Just head to Facebook's Home page at www.facebook.com, type

the email address you used to register in the **Email** box, type your
password in the **Password** box, and click **Log In**. Facebook logs you
in and displays your Home page, which features your News Feed and
provides access to the rest of Facebook from one convenient location.
To exit Facebook, click the down arrow in the upper-right corner of
the screen and click **Log Out**.

Enter your email address and password to log on.

WHOA!

If someone else has access to your computer, don't let your browser
remember your password and log out when you're done on Facebook.
Otherwise, someone can easily log in, read the discussions you're
having with your friends, view your photos and videos, and post status
updates pretending they're coming from you. Others can even change
your password, preventing *you* from logging in! Another option is,
when you're logging in, deselect the option **Keep me logged in** (if it's
checked) before clicking the **Log In** button. That way, Facebook logs you
out automatically when you exit.

In Your Face with the Interface

When you log in, Facebook gets in your face with all the buttons,
bars, links, icons, and menus you need to access everything.
Facebook has done a nice job of organizing all this stuff, but the
interface can seem a little overwhelming at first. Here, we highlight
the main areas you need to focus on and describe them in more
detail in the sections that follow. If you don't see a screen with this
stuff on it, click **Home** (in the top menu).

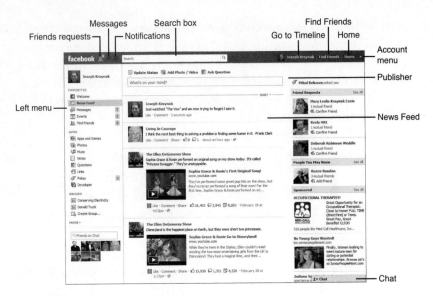

Facebook's interface.

Scooting Up to the Top Menu

The top menu (the blue bar) is Old Reliable. It appears at the top of the window no matter where you are or what you're doing on Facebook, providing quick access to the following features (from left to right on the bar):

- **Facebook:** Clicking the Facebook icon takes you Home— to the page that greets you when you sign on.

- **Friend Requests:** Click the **Friend Requests** icon, and a menu drops down, displaying any Facebook members who are asking to be your friend. The menu also contains a Find Friends link you can click to search for your friends on Facebook. See Chapter 4 for more about friends.

- **Messages:** Click the **Messages** icon, and Facebook displays a list of any messages you received. The menu also contains the Send a New Message link you can click to compose and send a message. See Chapter 6 for more about Facebook's Message feature.

- **Notifications:** Click the **Notifications** icon to view a list of your Facebook friends' current activities that pertain to you. Facebook notifies you whenever someone sends you a message, posts something on your Timeline or Wall, or comments on something you commented on. (See "Adjusting Your Account Settings" later in this chapter to find out how to configure how and how often Facebook notifies you.)

- **Search:** Click in the **Search** box, type a search word or phrase, and press **Enter** or **Return** on your computer keyboard to search Facebook for people, places, things, or help with a particular feature.

- **<Your Name>:** Click **<Your Name>** to display your Timeline, where you can post and access information about yourself, your photo albums, and other items of interest. In Chapter 3, you learn how to edit your Timeline. In Chapter 5, you discover how to communicate with your Facebook friends' Timelines or Walls.

- **Find Friends:** Click **Find Friends**, and Facebook takes you to your Friends page, which contains any friend requests you've received along with tools to help you track down people you know on Facebook. (You can send friend requests to people who aren't Facebook members, but they'll have to join Facebook to accept your request.)

- **Home:** Click **Home**, and Facebook takes you to your Home page—the same place you end up if you click **facebook** on the left end of the blue bar.

- **Down arrow:** The down arrow on the far right end of the blue bar opens the Account menu, which provides access to several options: Account Settings, Privacy Settings, Log Out, and Help. Later in this chapter, we provide additional details on changing your account settings and getting help. Chapter 2 shows you how to change Facebook's privacy settings.

Catching Up on Your News Feed

The News Feed is the core component of Facebook, providing you with a running account of just about everything you and your Facebook friends and the business, brands, and organizations you like are up to and have agreed to share with one another. (In Chapter 2, you learn how to change your privacy settings if you want to share less.)

You can sort your News Feed to display Top News or Most Recent by clicking **Sort** just above the News Feed and clicking the desired sort order. Top News displays a list of what Facebook deems are the most interesting posts from your Facebook friends. Most Recent displays all your friends' posts, starting with the most recent.

Checking Out the Publisher

At the top of your News Feed is your own personal Publisher. Whenever you want to post something to your News Feed, click in the Publisher's text box (the box containing "What's on your mind?"), type your message, and click **Post**. In addition to text messages, you can post photos, videos, links, or a question to poll your friends and see what they think. See Chapter 5 for a thorough explanation of the Publisher.

Exploring the Left Menu

The left menu (to the left of the News Feed) contains links for the most popular features on Facebook, including the following:

- **You:** At the top of the left menu is your Profile picture (assuming you added one) and your name. Click your photo or name, and Facebook displays your Timeline. See Chapter 3 for more about your Timeline. Click **Update Info** to change information you've entered about yourself.
- **Core features:** The next section down provides links to gain quick access to the four core Facebook features: News Feed, Messages, Events, and Find Friends. You find out more about all these features in later chapters.

- **Apps:** This section contains links to Facebook's collection of applications and games, along with links to popular Facebook applications ("apps," for short), including Photos, Music, Notes, and Questions.

- **Groups:** Below the Apps is a Groups section that initially contains only one option: Create Group. As you join or create groups, links for them appear here.

- **Chat:** At the bottom of the left menu are profile photos of friends in which you can message or chat. Click the photo of a Facebook friend with whom you want to chat, and a window pops up enabling you to type a message and send it to the person on Facebook or via a mobile phone.

Exploring the Column on the Right

The column on the right contains a hodgepodge of items of varying importance, including upcoming events, people you might know, and sponsored ads or announcements.

Checking Out the Ticker—If You Have One

If you're very active on Facebook, it rewards you with a *Ticker*—a window that streams all of your Facebook friends' activities, so you know immediately what your friends are up to on Facebook. If you're not active on Facebook, you won't see the Ticker, because Facebook figures that it won't do you much good.

Adjusting Your Account Settings

Facebook provides all sorts of ways to customize your experience, and it divides your options into two categories: Account Settings and Privacy Settings. In Chapter 2, we tackle privacy issues and show you how to tweak your privacy settings to share more or less information in accordance with your personal preferences.

To change your account settings, click the down arrow (upper-right corner) and then **Account Settings**. Navigate the following tabs to enter your preferences.

- **General:** Most items on the General tab let you change information you entered when you registered with Facebook—your name, username, email address, and password. You can also link your account to other accounts, including Google, MySpace, Yahoo!, and myOpenID, so when you log in to those accounts, you're automatically logged in to Facebook.

- **Security:** The Security settings protect against unauthorized access to your Facebook account.

  - **Security Question:** Add a security question to your account, so if someone hijacks your account and changes your password, you can more easily regain access to your account. (After you enter your security question, this option disappears and is no longer available, so if you don't see it, that's probably what happened.)

  - **Secure Browsing:** Enables you to access Facebook over a secure https connection, like the connection used on most sites for processing credit card transactions.

  - **Login Notifications:** Tells Facebook to notify you whenever someone logs in to your account from a computer you haven't used to log in before.

  - **Login Approvals:** Tells Facebook to prompt for a security code each time you log in.

  - **App Passwords:** Lets you require a password for any Facebook apps you use.

  - **Recognized Devices:** Lets you manage any devices you've registered to use with Facebook.

  - **Active Sessions:** Shows locations where you are currently logged in, so you can tell whether someone is logged in to your Facebook account from somewhere else.

- **Notifications:** Whenever just about anything happens on Facebook that involves you, Facebook can send a notification to the email address you used to register your account. You can use the options on the Notifications tab to enable or disable these email notifications for certain actions. (You can always see your notifications by logging on to Facebook and clicking the **Notifications** icon near the left end of the top menu.)

- **Subscribers:** Subscribers enables Facebook members who are not Facebook friends to follow you on Facebook. If you choose to allow subscribers, a Subscribe button appears on your public profile that any Facebook member can click to subscribe to your public posts. This enables you to broaden your reach, if desired, without friending anybody and everybody.

- **Apps:** When you click the Apps tab, Facebook displays a list of all apps you have authorized to interact with your Facebook account. Click **Edit** next to an app to access its settings, which vary depending on the app. For more about Facebook apps, check out Chapter 12.

- **Mobile:** The Mobile tab provides options to enable or disable Facebook for use with your smartphone or other mobile device. Enabling the mobile features allows Facebook to send notifications to your phone and allows you to access Facebook from your mobile phone. For more about using Facebook with your cell phone or smartphone, check out Chapter 14.

- **Payments:** Don't panic! Facebook is free. However, if you engage in business transactions, such as buying gifts for your friends or purchasing online advertising, you can click the **Payments** tab to enter payment preferences (Visa, MasterCard, and so on) and choose your preferred currency (dollar, euro, yen, and so on) for displaying prices and credit card charges.

- **Facebook Ads:** If you're concerned about your name or photo showing up in an advertisement on Facebook, click the **Facebook Ads** tab to learn more about what Facebook allows and prohibits in terms of advertisers using member information. This page includes links you can click to view current ad settings and change the settings, if desired, to control how Facebook uses or may use your information now or in the future. For more about advertising on Facebook, check out Chapter 18.

FRIEND-LY ADVICE

If you're tired of being notified every time one of your friends sneezes on Facebook, head to the Notifications settings to make some adjustments.

Following Facebook Rules and Etiquette

To flourish as a social-networking utility, Facebook must provide enough freedom to allow members to express themselves, find one another, and exchange information, but not so much freedom that members are subject to harassment or having their personal information published or read without their permission. As a result, Facebook has some rules for members to follow and etiquette guidelines to help members police their own behaviors.

Rules and Regulations

Facebook sets the rules that govern membership in its Terms of Service, which you can read in its entirety by scrolling down to the footer and clicking **Terms**. They basically boil down to the following do's and don'ts:

- Do provide accurate and current information in your Profile.
- Don't use Facebook to do anything illegal, immoral, or unethical.
- Do respect the rights of other members.
- Don't spam.

- Don't collect user information for marketing purposes without Facebook's permission.
- Don't do anything malicious to Facebook, including uploading viruses or unleashing denial-of-service attacks.

Etiquette

In the world of social networking, the rules of etiquette carry about as much weight as the Terms of Service. They protect others not only from being exposed to ill-mannered behavior, but also from the embarrassment that often follows from failing to act in accordance with a community's social norms. Following are several etiquette guidelines every Facebook member should follow:

- Include a current, realistic, socially acceptable photo of yourself and only yourself in your Profile. Don't use a photo of a pet, your favorite superhero, a shot with your significant other, or a group photo.
- Proofread your Profile and status updates before posting information.
- Respond to status updates regularly. You don't have to comment on every status update, but do express genuine interest in what's going on in your friends' lives.
- Don't friend just anybody. It cheapens your true friendships and could potentially expose your friends and what they say to people they'd rather not know. In addition, you may be judged by the company you keep and what that company shares on your Timeline and in your News Feed.
- Don't over-poke. It gets annoying really fast. (Poking consists of pulling up a friend's Profile by clicking on her name or photo and then clicking the **Poke** link (upper right of the page last we checked). The recipient of the poke receives a message letting her know you've acknowledged her existence. It's kind of dopey, which is why you should do it rarely, if at all.

- Ask for permission before tagging someone in a photo. More about tagging photos in Chapter 7.

- Watch your language. If you wouldn't say it front of your mom or your boss, don't say it on Facebook.

- If you're on Facebook to promote yourself or your business, do so in the acceptable venues, including a Facebook page and ads, not by posting promotional content to your Facebook friends' News Feeds or Timelines.

Help! Navigating Facebook's Help System

Although we cover the most important stuff you need to know to use Facebook, we can't cover everything in such a limited space and, as explained in the introduction, Facebook is in a constant state of change. If you need help with something that's not covered in this book or that has changed since we wrote about it, head to Facebook's Help system. Click the down arrow (upper-right corner) and click **Help** or click the **Help** link at the bottom of any Facebook page. The Help link takes you directly to the Facebook Help Center. If you click the down arrow and click **Help**, Facebook displays a drop-down menu asking what you need help with, providing links to common help topics, and displaying a Go to Help Center button.

The Facebook Help Center enables you to search for a keyword or question, browse help topics and discussions, view the top questions and their answers, and brush up on Facebook safety and privacy.

To search for a specific answer, click in the **Enter a keyword or question** box, type a search phrase that best expresses the question you have or the feature you need assistance with, and click the magnifying glass icon or press Enter or Return. (As you type, a list of help topics appears that match what you type appears, and you can click on the topic that's most relevant.) If you typed a word or phrase and clicked the magnifying glass icon or pressed Enter or Return, Facebook displays a collection of links that most closely match your search. Click the link you think is most likely to provide the information you need.

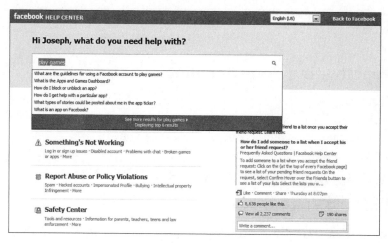

Search Facebook Help.

To browse for help, click a link for the type of help you need, such as Facebook Basics, and then follow the trail of links to the solution.

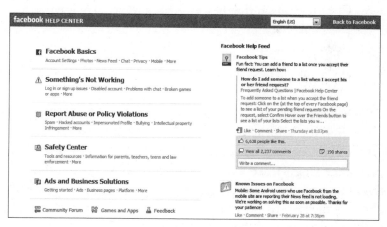

Browse Facebook's Help Topics.

Quitting Facebook

For whatever reason, should you decide that you want out of Facebook, you have two exits: you can deactivate your account or delete it.

Deactivating Your Account

Deactivating your account leaves all your stuff intact. If you quit and get homesick for Facebook, you can always pick up where you left off. To deactivate your account, here's what you do:

1. Click the down arrow button (upper-right corner) and click **Account Settings**.

2. Click the **Security** tab.

3. Below the list of security settings, click **Deactivate your account**. Facebook displays the guilt screen, complete with photos of all the friends who will miss you very, very much. Don't look.

4. Scroll down the page to the deactivation options.

5. Click the reason that best describes why you're leaving Facebook.

6. (Optional) Click in the **Please explain further** box and type any additional explanation you'd like to pass along to the folks at Facebook. (Be nice, or at least respectful.)

7. (Optional) If you want to stop receiving email notifications from Facebook whenever your friends invite you to do something or send you a message, click **Opt out of receiving future emails from Facebook**.

8. Click the **Confirm** button. Facebook deactivates your account and displays a message informing you how to return later if you change your mind.

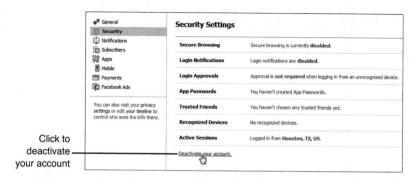

Click to
deactivate
your account

Deactivate your Facebook account.

Deleting Your Account

Deleting an account is a more serious and long-term decision. Everything in your account is erased, including your photos, notes, list of friends, and so on. It's like getting rid of all your stuff and entering a witness-protection program.

If you're sure you want to delete your account, it's pretty simple. Head to https://www.facebook.com/help/delete_account, click the **Delete My Account** button, and respond to any confirmation warnings as desired. You're outta there.

Delete your Facebook account.

The Least You Need to Know

- To get on Facebook, go to www.facebook.com and then complete the Sign Up form and submit it.

- Your News Feed shows status updates, photos, videos, and other stuff that you and your friends have chosen to share.

- To post something to your News Feed, click in the Publisher (top of the News Feed), type something, and click **Post**.

- To view your Timeline, click your profile photo or name in the blue bar at the top of any Facebook screen.

- To return to the opening page, click the **Facebook** logo on the left end of the top menu or **Home** on the right end.

- You can get help at any time by clicking the down arrow (upper-right corner of any Facebook screen) and then **Help**.

Protecting Your Privacy

In This Chapter

- Restricting access to your personal information
- Banning certain members from contacting you
- Protecting yourself from phishers, hackers, spammers, and other lowlifes
- Keeping your email address from falling into the wrong hands

Before you bare your soul on Facebook, you should be aware of just how private and secure your information is likely to be and any threats that might be lurking on or beyond your Timeline. Fortunately, Facebook provides several features that enable you to control access to the information you choose to share and with whom. This chapter covers key privacy and security concerns and shows you how to protect yourself and any sensitive information on Facebook.

Setting Your Privacy Preferences

Although Facebook is open to the public, your life doesn't need to be. Facebook provides privacy settings you can use to restrict or allow access to your information and activities on Facebook. By default, only your Facebook friends have access to most of your Timeline and can see your status updates and various activities you engage in.

In addition, Facebook *never* discloses pokes (except to the person you poke), messages (except to the recipient), whose Timeline or photos you view, whose notes you read, groups and events you decline to join, friend requests you ignore or reject, friends you remove, or notes and photos you delete.

> **WHOA!**
>
> Although Facebook provides plenty of settings for restricting access to your information, people you choose to share information with could share your information with others, so you still need to be careful. Share with care.

To access your privacy settings, click the down arrow (top right corner of the screen) and click **Privacy Settings**. The Privacy Settings page appears, presenting several groups of related privacy options, along with Blocked People and Apps to prevent certain people and Apps from contacting you on Facebook or accessing your information. We cover these options in the following sections.

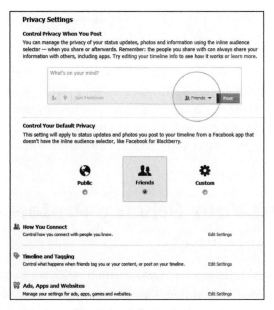

The Privacy Settings page.

Facebook has a long track record of changing the way you access privacy options, so remain flexible. You're likely to encounter the same options described in the following sections, but how you access those options may differ.

How You Connect

To tighten or relax restrictions on who can look you up using your email address or phone number or send you friend requests or messages, access your Privacy Settings page and then, next to How You Connect, click **Edit Settings**. This displays the How You Connect dialog box.

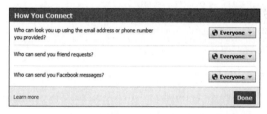

You can tighten or relax restrictions on how people can find and contact you.

When you're done entering your preferences in the Custom Privacy dialog box, click **Done**.

Timeline and Tagging

You and your friends can post to each other's Timeline and tag one another in status updates, photos, or videos. However, you might not always (or ever) want certain friends posting to your Timeline or knowing where you are or have been, with whom, and what you were doing, so Facebook gives you control of your Timeline and the way tags related to you are shared.

To control your Timeline and tags, access the Privacy Settings page and then next to Timeline and Tagging, click **Edit Settings**. The Timeline and Tagging dialog box appears, enabling you to change the following settings:

- **Who can post on your timeline?** You can choose to allow Facebook friends or no one to post to your Timeline.

- **Who can see what others post to your timeline?** You can choose to share your Timeline with everyone, only your Facebook friends, your Facebook friends and their friends, or choose Custom to share only with specific individuals or friend lists. (For more about friends and friend lists, see Chapter 4.)

- **Review posts friends tag you in before they appear on your timeline:** Turn on this setting if you want to review items in which you've been tagged before they're posted to your Timeline.

- **Who can see posts you've been tagged in on your timeline?** You can choose to share posts in which you've been tagged with everyone, only your Facebook friends, your Facebook friends and their friends, or choose Custom to share only with specific individuals or friend lists.

- **Review tags friends add to your own posts on Facebook:** Turn on this setting if you want to be able to review tags that your Facebook friends try to add to your posts.

- **Who sees tag suggestions when photos that look like you are uploaded?** Whenever someone posts a photo that contains someone Facebook thinks you look like, suggestions are sent to you and others to tag you in the photo. This option lets you choose who sees those suggestions. You can choose Friends or No One.

Ads, Apps, and Websites

Certain advertisements, applications, and websites require access to your Facebook information to do whatever it is they do, such as getting you registered or logged in. Here's a summary of the types of information Facebook gives ads, applications, and websites access to and the activities that trigger these permissions:

- If you or one of your friends visits an application or a Facebook-enhanced website, the application or website can access only the information in your public profile—your name, networks, profile picture, and friend list—plus any information you choose to make available to "everyone." (A Facebook-enhanced website is one that Facebook does not own or operate but that interfaces with the Facebook platform on a permission basis.)

- When you authorize an application (see Chapter 13), you give it permission to access any information in your account that it requires to work, except for your contact information.

- Facebook requires that applications and websites honor all of your privacy settings.

- If a friend authorizes an application, it can access any information in her account that it requires to work, including your friend's friend list. This means even if you don't authorize the application, it has permission to access some of your information, too, specifically your name, Profile picture, gender, networks, user ID, and any other information you've chosen to make accessible to everyone, unless you turn off platform applications and websites, as explained later in this section.

- If you performed an action that's relevant to a certain advertisement, such as your choosing to like a certain product, your confirmed Facebook friends may be able to see that action alongside the ad.

- If you visit a Facebook-enhanced website, it may access information in accordance with the previous rules in this list. If you choose not to proceed with a Facebook action on an external website, Facebook deletes any information about you that the site may have collected and sent back to Facebook.

You can restrict ad, application, and website access to some of your information by adjusting their privacy settings. Head to the Privacy page and next to Ads, Apps and Websites, click **Edit Settings**. Use the available buttons to enter your preferences.

You can restrict ad, app, and website access to your information.

On the Apps, Games and Websites privacy page, you can change the privacy settings for the following options:

- **Apps you use:** You can click **Remove** to remove apps you no longer use, click **Turn off** to turn off one or more platform apps, or click **Edit Settings** to adjust privacy settings for specific applications. (A platform app is an application that runs on Facebook.) If you don't want to use Facebook apps or websites, share information with them, or share information with them through your friends' accounts, click **Turn off all apps**, click **Select all**, and click **Turn Off Apps**.

- **How people bring your info to apps they use:** Your Facebook friends may share information about you with an application or Facebook-enhanced external website. For example, your friend may use a greeting card application that gathers the names and birthdays of all her friends to prompt her to send a card on her friend's birthday.

To prevent your friends from sharing certain pieces of information about you, click **Edit Settings**, remove the checkbox next to every piece of information you *don't* want your friends passing along, and click **Save Changes**.

- **Instant personalization:** Instant personalization is designed to improve your experience in Facebook's partner sites—for example, by enabling you to interact with Facebook friends who might be visiting the site at the same time and viewing your friends' movie ratings or travel advice on sites that offer those features. If you don't want Facebook sharing your information with these sites, click **Edit Settings** next to Instant personalization, click the checkbox next to **Enable instant personalization on partner websites**, and click **Confirm**.

- **Public search:** If someone searches for you on Google, Yahoo!, or another search site, the site may display a preview of your Timeline. You can use this option to disable public search, so if people want to find you on Facebook, they need to search on Facebook.

- **Ads:** Facebook allows you to adjust settings for third-party and social ads. Third-party ad settings enable you to prohibit third-party ads from including your name or profile picture, if Facebook chooses to allow this in the future. With social ad settings, you can tell Facebook to pair your social actions with ads for only your friends or no one.

Blocking People, Invitations, and Apps

Certain people and activities can become annoying on Facebook, particularly if you have friends who love to play games and aren't happy until all of their friends are playing those same games. Fortunately, Facebook enables you to block individuals, group and event invitations, and apps that become more annoying than engaging.

To block a person or activity, go to the Privacy Settings page, scroll down to Blocked People and Apps, click **Manage Blocking**, and use the resulting options to enter your preferences. If you choose to block someone, Facebook doesn't notify the person of the block, because that would be downright rude. (You can block a person by email address, instead, which comes in handy if the person isn't a Facebook member yet. Just use the Email box instead of the Name box.)

Choose Your Privacy Settings ▸ Manage Blocking

◀ Back to Privacy

Add friends to your Restricted list	When you add friends to your Restricted list they can only see the information and posts that you make public. Facebook does not notify your friends when you add them to your Restricted list. Edit List.
Block users	Once you block someone, that person can no longer be your friend on Facebook or interact with you (except within apps and games you both use and groups you are both a member of).

Name: Charles Manson   Block

Email: Block

You haven't added anyone to your block list.

Block app invites	Once you block app invites from someone, you'll automatically ignore future app requests from that friend. To block invites from a specific friend, click the "Ignore All Invites From This Friend" link under your latest request.

Block invites from: Type the name of a friend…

Block event invites	Once you block event invites from someone, you'll automatically ignore future event requests from that friend.

Block invites from: Type the name of a friend…

Block apps	Once you block an app, it can no longer contact you or get non-public information about you through Facebook. Learn More.

Block apps: Type the name of an app…

Block a person, group, or event invitations, or an app.

Another way to block a person is to pull up her Timeline, click the button with the asterisk–like symbol on it (in the upper-right corner of the person's screen), and click the **Report/Block**. The **Report and/or Block This Person** dialog box appears, and you can choose to block the person, report the individual (be sure to select a reason), unsubscribe from the person's Timeline, or unfriend the person.

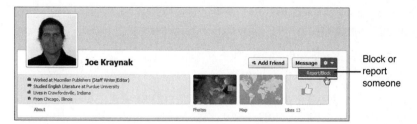

You can block or report someone.

WHOA!

Removing someone from your blocked list doesn't automatically restore your friendship. If you want to take the person back as a friend, you'll need to send him a new friend request and grovel for his approval, as discussed in Chapter 4.

Defending Yourself from Hackers and Phishers

Facebook does a fairly good job of policing activity and cracking down on inappropriate behavior, but hackers, stalkers, schemers, and scammers have been known to ply their trade on Facebook. To protect yourself, your information, and your account from these miscreants, you should be aware of the potential threats and practice some safe Facebooking strategies.

Keeping Hackers from Hijacking Your Account

A malicious hacker may be able to hijack your Facebook account and then pose as you. Once she gains access, she can do anything from posting tasteless jokes in your News Feed to emailing your friends requesting a money transfer or credit card information so you can fly back home from Bora Bora, where you've been robbed and held captive for 36 hours.

To protect your account and information from hackers, consider practicing the following safeguards:

- Check and adjust your account security settings, as explained in Chapter 1.

- Change your password to something that's difficult for hackers and nosy bodies to guess. Include both letters and numbers, and make it fairly long—10 to 14 characters are better than 6 to 8. Use a different password than you use for other online accounts. Remember, passwords are case sensitive. To access the form for changing your password, click the down arrow (top-right corner), **Account Settings**, **General**, and then, across from Password, click **Edit**.

- If other people have access to the computer you use to log in to Facebook, log out whenever you're done using Facebook. Also, don't use your browser's "remember" feature to store your username and password.

- Include as little sensitive information as possible in your Profile; if a hacker does gain access, he won't have your name, address, phone number, and other potentially sensitive information.

- Don't give your login information to anyone for any reason. Hackers may pose as Facebook representatives to trick you into passing along your login information. See the next section, "Dodging Phishing Schemes," for details.

FRIEND-LY ADVICE

If your account has been hijacked, try logging in to Facebook and changing your password. If the hacker already changed your password so you can't log in, go to www.facebook.com, click the **Forgot your password?** link, and follow the on-screen instructions to reset your password. You must have access to one of the email accounts associated with your Facebook account, so Facebook can send you a new password. If you don't have access to one of those email accounts, you can use your security question/answer to regain access to your Facebook account.

Dodging Phishing Schemes

Phishing schemes dangle a line in front of you, hoping you'll take the bait. In this case, the bait is usually an email alert warning you of some problem with your account. The alert typically contains a link you can click to go to a site where you can learn more and address the issue. The site looks official and matches what you expect to see—in this case, a Facebook-like interface. You think you're on Facebook, but you're really on a website the phisher created and, before you can fix the problem, you have to log in.

Unfortunately, if you do try to log in, you pass your Facebook login information directly to the phisher, who can then log in to your real Facebook account, change your password, access your information, pose as you, and cause all sorts of trouble.

To defend yourself against phishing schemes, practice the following maneuvers:

- Trust your instincts. If something looks or sounds phishy or too good to be true, it probably is.

- Keep in mind that just because something appears to be coming from an official source or a friend, it might not be. Anyone can pose as an official source, and a friend's account may have been hijacked.

- If you receive an alert via the web or email, compare the URL in the link with the one that appears in your browser or email program's status bar when you rest the mouse pointer on the link. The link might show www.facebook. com but take you to an entirely different site. You can tell where a link is really going to take you by hovering the mouse pointer over the link and looking in the status bar.

- Keep in mind that Facebook will never send you an email message asking for your login information. Anyone who's asking for it is probably a bad guy.

- If it looks as though someone has hijacked a friend's account and is posing as him, contact your friend immediately, and whatever you do, don't comment on or "like" a suspicious status update, and certainly don't ever click on a link of a suspicious nature.

- Report any suspected phishing schemes to Facebook so management can investigate and shut down the perpetrators. At the top of every message you receive is a Report link you can click to report the suspicious message to Facebook. More details about reporting Facebook violations are provided later in this chapter.

Preventing and Stopping Spam

We haven't seen a great deal of spam on Facebook, probably because the service and its members do such a fine job of policing members and advertisers. If you do receive a message on Facebook that appears to be spam, open the **Actions** menu near the top of the message screen, click **Report as Spam**, and follow the on-screen instructions to report the spammer.

Keep in mind that if you're receiving spam that has supposedly originated from a Facebook friend, your friend's account probably has been hijacked.

Reporting Scams and Schemes to Facebook

Facebook monitors members and the activities they engage in, but it relies on members like you to call attention to any abuse of the service. If you notice any lewd, crude, or potentially criminal activity on Facebook, report it. Following are various ways to file a report:

- **Click a Report link and follow the on-screen instructions.** Facebook displays the Report link in various places, including in the Action menu above any open messages, above photos, in notes, and in groups.
- **Email abuse@facebook.com.** You can send an email message to Facebook to report suspected member violations.
- **Email advertise@facebook.com.** Send an email message to report any suspected abuse by advertisers on Facebook.

When notifying Facebook of suspected violations, be as specific as possible. Identify the member or advertiser by name and describe the violation and where you observed it. Provide a link or URL (page address), if possible.

The Least You Need to Know

- Check and adjust your privacy settings. Know what you're sharing, and restrict access to anything you don't want to share.
- To access the privacy settings, click the down arrow in the upper-right corner of any Facebook page, and then click **Privacy Settings**.
- Consider removing your home address and phone number from your Profile and not sharing your email address with anyone.
- Keep hackers at bay by using a password that's tough to guess and tightening your account's security settings, as explained in Chapter 1.
- Never click a link in a message or post and then enter your username and password or other sensitive information; it could be a phishing scam.
- Report any violations or suspicious activity to Facebook.

Navigating the Facebook Timeline

In This Chapter

- Grasping Timeline basics
- Navigating and personalizing your Timeline
- Checking out other Facebook members' Timelines
- Subscribing to a Facebook member's posts

Almost everyone on Facebook has a *Timeline*—a scrapbook that documents each member's life, from the day he was born to the here and now, utilizing a visual timeline that runs down the middle of your personal Facebook page. You can add a cover image at the top of your Timeline, add life events such as your high school graduation or your wedding day, map the places you've been, and much more. As you post updates, interact with others, and use apps, Facebook keeps a running record of your activities on your Timeline. In addition, Facebook friends can post to one another's Timelines to engage in conversations.

This chapter takes you on a Timeline tour and shows you how to personalize your Timeline and interact with other Facebook members' Timelines, and subscribe to the content they post.

What?! No Timeline?!

As of this writing, Facebook was still rolling out the Timeline user interface, so you or some of your friends might not have it yet. If you see "Profile" in the blue bar at the top of the screen, instead of your name and profile picture, you don't have the Timeline. If you access a friend's page and see "Wall" near the top of the left column, your friend doesn't have the Timeline.

If you don't have the Timeline, it's easy enough to get. Log in to Facebook, click **Profile** in the blue bar at the top or click your name or profile picture in the column on the left, and Facebook displays a message at the top of your Profile indicating that you don't have the Timeline. Click the link to get the Timeline. (Another option is to head to Facebook's Timeline page at www.facebook.com/about/timeline and click **Get Timeline**.)

However you get the Timeline, you can then personalize it as explained in this chapter. After personalizing it, click the **Publish** button to put it into action.

If someone doesn't have the Timeline, she has a Profile and a Wall instead. The Profile is like the About section of the Timeline, presenting information about the person, and the Wall is like the Timeline itself—a place where friends can share content with one another in a quieter place than the News Feed. If a Facebook friend hasn't transitioned to the Timeline, you might still find yourself dealing with the friend's Profile and Wall.

Navigating Your Timeline

To access your Timeline, click your profile picture or your name in the blue bar at the top of any Facebook screen. At first glance, your Timeline might look like a disjointed collage. The following list breaks the timeline down into its many components to add some order to the apparent chaos:

- **Cover:** This big block at the top of the page contains the cover image, your profile picture, "about" information, and thumbnails for one-click access to your Friends, Photos,

Likes, and any Facebook apps you choose to add to this area.

- **Timeline navigator:** The timeline navigator, in the right column, lets you quickly scroll to a specific month or year in the Timeline.

- **Timeline Publisher:** The Timeline Publisher lets you and your friends post content to your Timeline. Friends can post updates, photos, or places. You can post all of that, plus life events, such as getting married, adopting a pet, and more.

- **Friends:** This box displays photos and names of several friends along with a **See All** link you can click to access your entire collection of Facebook friends.

- **The actual time *line*:** The line that runs down the middle of the page represents your entire life. Hover the mouse pointer over the line and a plus sign appears. Click the plus sign and the Publisher toolbar appears, enabling you to add a status update, photo/video, place, or life event to the Timeline.

- **Stories:** These are the boxed items on either side of the time line. If you look at your Timeline as a scrap book, these are the scraps that document your life and activities on and off Facebook in photographs, maps, video, and other media. Hover the mouse pointer over a story to display buttons in the story's upper-right corner for featuring the story or editing it. If you feature a story, Facebook displays it in a wider box that spans both sides of the Timeline.

- **Feature/app thumbnails:** Just below the cover image are thumbnails for one-click access to your Facebook Friends, Photos, Likes, and Notes. Click the small button with the number in it to expand this area. Click the plus sign in the upper-right corner of an empty block to add a thumbnail for one of your favorite Facebook games or apps.

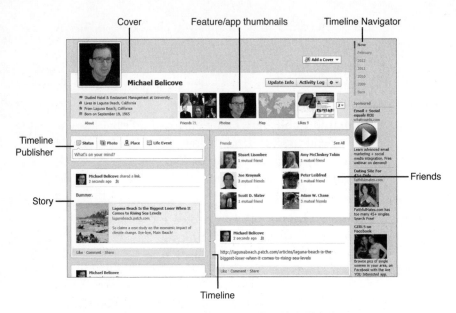

Familiarize yourself with your Facebook Timeline.

Enhancing and Embellishing Your Timeline

Whether you're just getting started or have been a Facebook member for several years, you should spend some time exploring what's on your Timeline and personalizing it. When people check you out on Facebook, your Timeline is what they see, so make sure it represents you the way you want to be represented. The following sections show you how.

Add or Modify a Cover Image

The first thing you'll want to do is add a cover image. Click **Add a Cover**, click **Choose from my photos** or **Upload a photo**, and use the resulting screen or dialog box to complete the task. You can then drag the cover to reposition it. When you're done, click **Save Changes**.

Personalize your Timeline with a cover image.

Edit Your Profile Picture

Your profile picture overlaps the lower left of your cover image and appears to the left of your status updates and the comments you leave on others' updates, photos, videos, and anywhere else you can leave a comment. To use a different picture, remove it, or reposition the thumbnail, hover the mouse pointer over your profile picture, click **Edit Profile Picture**, and choose the desired option. You can choose a new photo from one you've already uploaded, take a new photo with your webcam, upload a new photo, edit the thumbnail (scale it to fit within the frame and reposition it in the frame), or remove the photo altogether.

FRIEND-LY ADVICE

To add a baby picture, click **Born** at the bottom of the Timeline navigator (in the right column), click **+ Add a Photo** (just below your birthday), and use the resulting options to choose or upload a photo and add details about where you were born, your parents, and the story of your birthday.

Edit Your Personal Information

To display a page for editing your personal information, which appears in the About section of your profile, click **About** (below the personal information highlights that are below your cover image). Use the resulting page to edit or enter any information you want to include about yourself.

For some items, you can change the privacy setting. Click the privacy button (the globe with the down arrow next to it) and choose **Public**, **Friends**, **Only me**, or **Custom** (to enter more specific settings).

Edit your personal information.

Post a Current or Past Event to Your Facebook Timeline

Chances are good that you have a huge gap in your Timeline between when you were born and now. To fill that gap, you need to post past events to your Timeline, such as your first birthday, high school graduation, and that wild night when you woke up the next morning with a tattoo.

To post a past or current event to your Timeline, use the Timeline Publisher. Click **Life Event**, click the category that most closely describes the event, such as **Work & Education** or **Travel & Experiences**, and then click the item on the resulting menu that most clearly describes the event, such as **New School** or **New Job**.

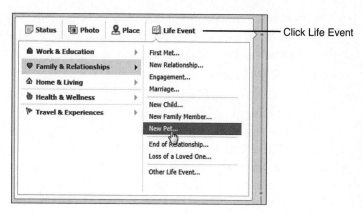

Click Life Event

Post a new life event to your Timeline.

A dialog box appears, prompting you to enter detailed information and perhaps other content, such as a photo. Enter the requested details, especially the date on which the event occurred. When you're finished, click **Save**.

WHOA!

When you post a life event to your Timeline, you share that event with others. To specify who can see the life event, head to your Timeline, click **About**, and then enter your preferences.

Another way to post a past event is to scroll down the Timeline to the year/month of the event, mouse over the actual time line so a plus sign appears, and click the plus sign. A floating Publisher appears, and you can post your event as described previously. The benefit here is that Facebook supplies the year and the month of the event for you, and all you need to do is choose the day.

Post Your Status, a Photo, or a Place to Your Facebook Timeline

You can also use your Timeline Publisher to post your status, a photo, or a place:

- **Status:** Click in the **What's on your mind?** box and type your entry.

- **Photo or video:** Click **Photo** and then click **Upload Photo/Video**, **Use Webcam**, or **Create Photo Album**, and use the resulting dialog box to upload or choose the desired photo or video.

- **Place:** Click **Place**, click in the **Where are you?** box, and start typing a place name (such as a business or school) and/or a city, state, or country or some other indication of where you are. As you type, Facebook displays the names of places that match what you've entered, and you can click one of the entries. If none of the locations listed is correct, scroll to the bottom of the list and click **Just use <whatever you entered>**.

At the bottom of the Timeline Publisher are additional options. You can click the person + icon to enter the names of Facebook friends you're with, click the pinpoint icon to specify your location, and use the drop-down menu to specify who will be allowed to view the post.

After entering the desired contents and settings, click **Post**.

Post a status update, photo, or place.

Share Interests on Your Timeline

The music you like to listen to, the books you read, the TV shows you watch, the teams you cheer for, and other activities and interests you engage in are a reflection of who you are and are often of interest to your Facebook friends, so consider sharing this information on your timeline. To share your interests, all you have to do is flag what you like. Head to your Timeline and click the **Likes** icon near the bottom of the cover area. Click the icon that best represents the category in which you want to post what you like: **Add Music**, **Add Books**, **Add TV Shows**, and so on. Use the resulting options to specify what you like. Click **Save Changes** when you're done.

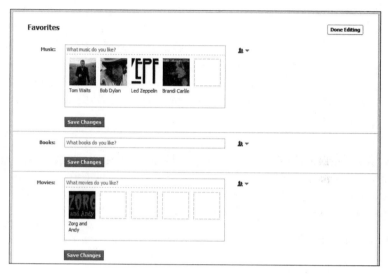

Share interests on your Timeline.

Edit Your Activity Log

Your activity log is your own private, unfiltered Facebook Timeline. It contains everything you've done on Facebook. You can edit your activity log to be more selective about what appears in your Facebook Timeline.

To edit your activity log, click **Activity Log** (just across from your cover image). Select the year you want to edit and, if desired, click **All** (upper right) and click the desired type of activity you want to focus on, such as photos or comments or likes.

To include or exclude an item from your Timeline, feature it on your Timeline, choose who can view it, or enter other settings that pertain to the item, click the menu button to the right of the activity, and choose the desired option.

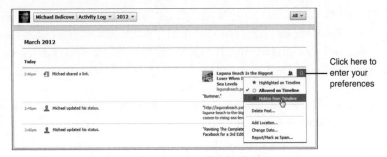

Click here to enter your preferences

Review and edit your activity log.

FRIEND-LY ADVICE

Browse your activity log and check the privacy settings for various types of information and specific entries to develop a better understanding of what you're sharing and not sharing. To find out what your Timeline looks like to someone else who's viewing it, click your name or profile photo in the blue bar at the top, click the button with the asterisk and down arrow on it next to the Activity Log button, and click **View As...** . Facebook displays the Timeline as it appears to the public. To see what it looks like to a specific Facebook friend, enter the friend's name in the **Enter a friend's name** box.

Mark Places You've Been on Your Map

If life is a journey, then your Timeline should certainly contain a log of where you've lived and traveled to. To add places you've lived and visited, click the **Map** icon below the cover image. Click in the **Where have you been?** box, type the name of a place you've been, and select the entry that's the closest match. A dialog box appears, prompting you to specify whether you were here, traveled here, or lived here. Click the appropriate answer, enter details into the resulting dialog box, and click **Save**.

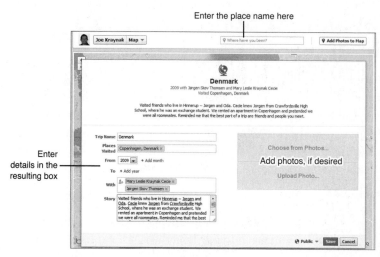

Enter the place name here

Enter details in the resulting box

Map places you've been.

Create a Thumbnail for an App

Below the cover image are thumbnails that provide quick access to your Friends List, Photos, Likes, Notes, and Subscriptions. To add a thumbnail for an app you frequently use, such as a game you play, click the arrow button, click a thumbnail that has a plus sign on it, and click the game or app you want to include. (If the arrow button has a number on it, that number represents how many items are not shown but will appear when you expand the area.)

You can move a thumbnail or remove it from the Featured area. Hover your mouse pointer over the thumbnail, click the edit button that appears, and click the desired option.

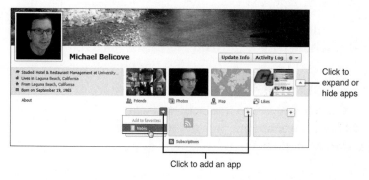

Click to expand or hide apps

Click to add an app

Add an app for quick access to it.

Navigating Someone Else's Timeline

A Facebook friend's Timeline is similar to yours, except you can't change the cover or edit the contents. Use the Timeline navigator, in the right column, to scroll to different periods in your friend's Timeline. Use the Timeline publisher to post status updates or photos to your friend's Timeline, including people you're with and the date and location.

Near the top of your friend's Timeline are several buttons:

✓ Friends Click **Friends** to open a drop-down menu that enables you to add your friend to a friend list, such as Close Friends or Acquaintances. You may also choose to unfriend the person. (For more about friends and friend lists, see Chapter 4.)

Suggest Friends Click **Suggest Friends** to display a window that contains a list of all of your friends. Click each friend you want to suggest to your friend, and click **Send Suggestions**.

Message Click **Message** to display a pop-up window near the bottom of your browser that enables you to send your friend a message (if your friend is not available for chat) or engage in chat if your friend is logged in to Facebook and available. For more about Facebook Messaging, see Chapter 6.

⚙ ▾ Open the tools menu for options to **See Friendship** to check out the ongoing dialog between you and your friend, **Poke** to acknowledge your friend's presence, **Add to Interest Lists** to create a custom News Feed of related posts, **Unfriend** this person, or **Report/Block** to report the person to Facebook or prevent the person from contacting you.

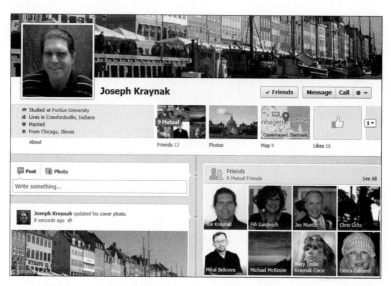

Navigate your friend's Timeline.

Near the bottom of the cover area are links you can click to access specific details about your friend, including personal information that your friend has chosen to share in the About section, your friend's friends, photos, likes, and notes.

When you access the Timeline of someone you haven't yet friended, what you see depends quite a bit on what the person chose to make public. However, you can expect to see one difference that's consistent regardless of what the person chose to make public—instead of a Friends button, the +1 Add Friend button appears, which you can click to send the person a friend request.

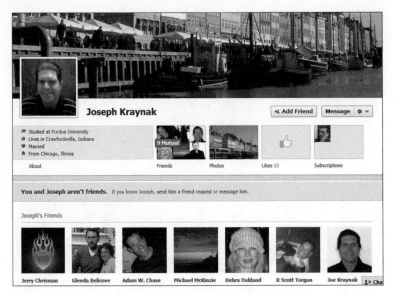

The Timeline of someone who's not yet your
Facebook friend.

Subscribing to and Unsubscribing from Timelines

Facebook's relatively new Subscribe feature enables you to view a person's posts even if you're not the person's Facebook friend, assuming the person has enabled this feature. Once you've subscribed to a person's posts, you can choose the type of content you want to view, such as life events, status updates, or comments and likes.

To subscribe, access the person's Timeline and click the **Subscribe** button. (If instead of Subscribe the button says "Subscribed," you're already subscribed.) Now, mouse over the **Subscribed** button for additional options. Click **Settings**. A drop-down menu appears, enabling you to receive more or fewer updates and subscribe to only specific content. Choose the number and type of updates you want to subscribe to. If no Subscribe button appears, the person has not enabled this feature.

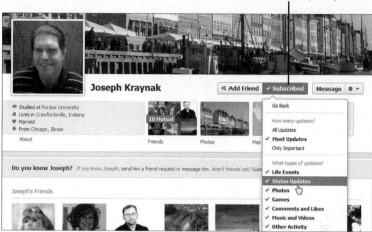

Enter your subscription preferences.

The Least You Need to Know

- To access your Timeline, click your name or profile picture in the blue bar at the top of any Facebook screen.

- Click **About**, lower left of your Timeline's cover area, to display personal information that you can edit.

- Click the **Subscribe** button on the Timeline of any Facebook member who has activated this feature to subscribe to the person's posts and have them appear in your News Feed. Click the **Subscribed** button for additional options.

- Mouse over the actual time line so a plus sign appears, and click to display a box for posting to the Timeline.

- Before posting anything, check to make sure you're sharing it only with people you want to see it: Public, Friends, Only Me, or Custom.

Finding and Friending People You Know

In This Chapter

- Scouring Facebook and beyond for people you know
- Friending Facebook members you know and love
- Unfriending people who no longer interest you
- Using friend lists to share selectively
- Exposing yourself to more potential friends

In real life, you're not just you. You are the sum total of yourself, your past, your aspirations, and everyone with whom you interact, including friends, family members, colleagues, and even those strangers you're about to meet.

The same is true on Facebook, only more so. When you first register and log in, all you are is a name. When you start to connect with friends, family members, colleagues, and former classmates—and they start connecting with you—you become part of a thriving community. Each new Facebook friend adds a stitch to the tapestry that's you. In short, to get anything *out of* Facebook, you need to get *into* Facebook and get connected. This chapter shows you how.

Knowing What It Means to Be a Friend

On Facebook, your friends have benefits that others on Facebook might not have, depending on your privacy settings (see Chapter 2). They can read your Timeline and follow discussions among you and your other friends, for example. When you "friend" someone on Facebook, you give him access to information about yourself and perhaps your friends that could be sensitive or confidential, so you'd better have a pretty clear idea of who your friends are and what you're sharing with them before you start adding people to your inner circle.

WHOA!

You have complete control over what appears on your Timeline and what's shared among friends, as explained in Chapters 2 and 3. Until you review your privacy settings and what you've chosen to share on your Timeline and your About page, choose your friends very carefully and assume everything you post is publicly accessible. If you receive a friend request from someone you don't know, ignore it for now.

Sharing Timelines and News Feeds

Friends share Timelines and News Feeds; that is, whatever you post to your News Feed is likely to show up on your friends' News Feeds and vice versa. If you add your mom as a friend, she'll be able to see whatever you post to your News Feed, and you'll see what she posts to hers. Post a message about the wild time you had at that party Friday night, and Mom can see it.

Your Timeline is a quieter place, displaying only your posts and anything your friends have specifically posted to your Timeline. In Chapter 5, you learn more about the News Feed and Timeline.

Sharing Photo Albums

When you upload photos to your account, your friends have access to those photos. You can restrict access to photos, as Chapter 7 explains, but until you learn how to do that, hold off on posting anything too risqué or revealing. Even if your photos are accessible only to your friends, they might decide to share those photos with others—some of whom you might not want looking at those photos.

Friends can also "tag" you in a photo that they or someone they know has uploaded to Facebook. Tagging means that the photo is labeled with your name and will link to your Timeline, which is kind of cool until someone tags you in an embarrassing pose or situation and that tag is broadcast to all your friends, family, and co-workers. (See Chapter 2 for guidance on how to control the way tags work on your Facebook account. In Chapter 7, you learn how to add and remove tags.)

Sharing Information

Unless you indicate otherwise, most of your About information is readily accessible to all your Facebook friends. This includes Basic Information, Personal Information, Contact Information (address, phone number, but not your email address, unless you choose to share it), Education and Work experience, and a list of any groups you've joined. (See Chapter 9 for more about the Groups feature.)

In Chapter 3, we explain how to edit the personal information on your About page and adjust privacy settings to hide sensitive information from prying eyes. Until then, become friends only with people you don't mind having access to your information.

Digging Up People You Know

The main purpose of Facebook is to facilitate connections among people, and because you have to find people before you can connect with them, Facebook features several ways to locate the people you know ... assuming, of course, they're on Facebook.

What about all those folks you know who aren't on Facebook yet? No worries—Facebook provides a way to invite them to join, assuming you have their email addresses!

After you make a few friends, Facebook might display friends of theirs and suggest that you invite them to be your friends. All you need to do is click the person's name in the Suggestions box or the "We'd like to help you find your friends" page, and follow the on-screen cues to send a friend request. More information on sending a friend request is provided later in this chapter.

Searching for an Individual by Name or Email

One of the easiest ways to dig up a specific individual on Facebook is to perform a search. Click in the **Search** box (in the blue bar at the top of any Facebook screen) and start typing the person's name or email address. As you type, the names of Facebook members appear that match what you've typed so far. If you see the person's name, click it to access the person's Profile page. You can then click the **Add Friend** button to send a friend request.

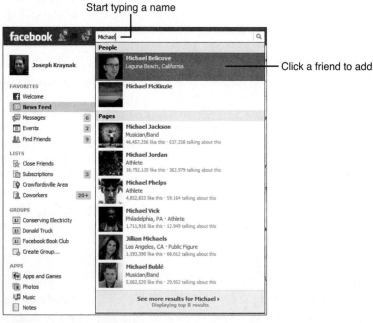

Search for a friend by name or email address.

If you finish typing and the person you're looking for doesn't pop up, press **Enter** or click the **Search** button (the magnifying glass to the right of the Search box). Facebook displays possible matches. If the person still doesn't show up, use another search method described in this chapter.

FRIEND-LY ADVICE

If you know the person's email address, try searching for that instead of the person's name. An email address is more likely to turn up the individual you're looking for and screen out all others with similar names.

Browsing for Friends

Facebook enables you to browse for friends from different parts of your life, including your hometown, current city, high school, or mutual friends. Click **Find Friends**, in the blue bar at the top. Facebook displays a list of people you might know based on information you entered about your hometown, your current location, schools you've attended, places you've worked, and so on.

POKE

Don't be surprised if your Find Friends screen differs from the one shown here. Facebook seemed to be transitioning to a new approach during the writing of the book. Your screen may display three sections: Requests, which you can confirm or not; Add Personal Contacts as Friends, which enables you to search for people you know using their email addresses, as explained in the next section; and People You May Know, whom you can choose to add as a friend, which is sort of like the screen shown here.

Click the check box next to each part of your life you want to use to filter the results. If you click the check box next to High School, for example, Facebook displays only those members who've indicated that they attended the same high school as you. Click the check boxes next to High School and Current City, and Facebook displays only those members who've indicated they attended the same high school *and* live in the same city as you.

To add another hometown, current city, high school, mutual friend, or whatever, click in the text box below the item you want to add, type your entry, and press Enter or Tab.

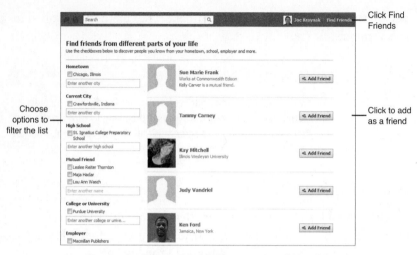

Browse for friends from different parts of your life.

WHOA!

Think twice about friending colleagues and co-workers. We've heard plenty of stories about co-workers passing along embarrassing and sometimes career-ending status updates that other co-workers and even the boss ended up reading. If you do friend a colleague, be especially careful about anything you post about your job, office politics, or other colleagues.

Searching for People in Your Email Address Book

Facebook can use your email address book to track down people you already keep in touch with. You can import addresses from a web-based email account, such as Google Mail or Yahoo! Mail, or directly from Microsoft Outlook. If you use some other email program or don't want to give Facebook access to your web-based email account, you can export the address book from your email program, save it as a file to your computer, and then import the addresses into Facebook.

Following are the steps for importing addresses from a web-based email program. (After these steps, we cover a couple variations you'll run into if you're using a different type of email program or would rather not give Facebook access to your web-based account.) Here's what you do:

1. Click in the **Search** box at the top of page, type **find friends**, and click **Find Friends**, which should be at the top of the list that appears.

2. Scroll down to the web-based email service you use and click **Find Friends** next to it. (If your email service isn't listed, click **Find Friends** next to Other Email Service.)

3. Enter the email address you use to log in to your web-based email program and click **Find Friends**. Facebook prompts you to enter your username and password for that service.

4. Enter your username and password for the web-based email service and click the button to sign in. Your service might display a prompt, through Facebook, asking you to confirm.

5. If prompted to confirm, click the option to give your okay. Facebook retrieves and then displays a list of any Facebook members who've registered using any of the email addresses in your address book.

6. Click the contacts you want to add as friends. (You can deselect contacts by clicking them again.)

7. Select any of your contacts not on Facebook that you want to invite. Facebook will invite nonmembers to become members so they can be your Facebook friends.

8. Click **Add Friends**. Facebook will email your friend request to everyone you selected.

FRIEND-LY ADVICE

In addition to finding people you email, Facebook can help you find people on popular services, including Skype.

Facebook can log in to your web-based email program
and import your email addresses.

If you have a PC running Windows and use Outlook, Outlook Express, or Windows Live Mail to manage your email, open the Find Friends page and next to Other Tools click **Find Friends**. Click **Upload Contact File**, click **Find My Windows Contacts**, and follow the on-screen prompts to complete the operation. Facebook scours your PC for a contacts file and displays a list of Facebook members who've registered with any of the addresses. Select the contacts you want to add as friends, click **Add Friends**, and follow the on-screen instructions to complete the operation.

If that didn't work or you use some other email client on your computer, such as Mozilla Thunderbird, next to Other Tools, click **Find Friends**, click **Upload Contact File**, and then click the **How to create a contact file …** link. This displays a list of links you can click for instructions on how to export an address book from any of several popular email programs. Click the link for your email program and follow the instructions to export your contact file.

After exporting your contact file, head back to your Find Friends page. Next to Other Tools, click **Find Friends**, click **Upload Contact File**, click **Choose File**, use the resulting dialog box to select the email address file you want to import, click **Open**, and then click **Upload Contacts**. Select the name of each person you want to invite to be your friend, and click **Add Friends**.

Befriending and Unfriending

Becoming friends on Facebook requires mutual consent. One member initiates the process by sending a friend request. The other member must then accept the invitation to confirm the arrangement.

In the following sections, you discover how to send and respond to friend requests, unfriend someone with whom you no longer want to associate, and group your friends using friend lists to help you navigate your various social circles.

Sending a Friend Request

You can bump into prospective friends all sorts of ways on Facebook. Someone can send you a friend request, you can track down the person by performing a search, your current friends can offer suggestions, or Facebook might display a list of suggested friends.

However you happen to bump into a person, the process for inviting them to become your friend is always the same: click **+1 Add Friend**.

In the past, a window would pop up that allowed you to add a personal message to the request and gave you a chance to cancel if you clicked the **+1 Add Friend** button just to see what would happen. Now, the request is sent immediately. If you need to cancel the request, head to the person's Timeline, click the **Friend Request Sent** button, and click **Cancel Request**. If the person already accepted your request, you'll have to unfriend the person, as explained later in this chapter. Your friend must confirm your request before Facebook establishes a connection.

Send a friend request to initiate a new friendship.

Responding to a Friend Request

When someone sends you a friend request, you might receive an email message with a link you can click to go to Facebook and respond to the request. If you don't check your email very often or have chosen not to receive email notifications (see Chapter 2), you can check for friend requests by logging on to Facebook and clicking the Friend Requests button in the top menu, just to the right of "facebook." (The button is barely visible if you have no recent friend requests. If you have recent friend requests, the button is highlighted and a number appears near it showing the number of new friend requests.)

When you click the Friend Requests button, a drop-down menu appears, displaying several of the most recent friend requests. At the bottom of the menu is the See All Friend Requests link, which you can click to display all friend requests on a separate page.

Every friend request includes the person's name and the number of friends you have in common, if any. You can click the person's name or photo to check out her Timeline or click the **mutual friends** link (if available) to find out which friends you have in common.

After accessing the Friend Requests list, you can click one of the following options to confirm or not:

- **Confirm**, to accept the invitation and become friends.
- **Not Now**, to disregard the invitation. This hides the invitation, and you can return to it later on your Friend Requests page. It also provides an option for deleting the request if you don't know the person. Don't worry, Facebook is polite. It doesn't send the person a rejection slip or anything like that.

YOU MAY ALSO LIKE...

The Complete Idiot's Guide to LinkedIn
by Susan Gunelius

Facebook All-in-One For Dummies
by Jamie Crager

Easy Facebook
by Michael Miller

My Facebook for Seniors
by Michael Miller

Facebook for Seniors QuickSteps
by Carole Matthews

If you're not sure whether you know the person, you can always send the person a message to find out how the person knows you and why he sent a friend request. Just click the person's name or photo to access his Timeline or Wall, click **Message**, and use the resulting dialog box to send your message. See Chapter 6 for more about Facebook's Messages feature.

You can confirm or ignore a friend request.

Dumping a Friend

If you've added a friend by mistake, or decide later that you really don't want the person hanging out in your Face-space, you can unfriend the person. Here's what you do:

1. Access your friend's Timeline.

2. Mouse over the **Friends** button and click **Unfriend**. A dialog box appears prompting you to confirm.

3. Click **Remove from Friends**.

FRIEND-LY ADVICE

Even though Facebook doesn't notify your friend of your decision to unfriend, it can result in an awkward situation if your former friend tries to post something to your Timeline or Wall and can't get to it. If you decide to re-friend, you have to go through the whole friend-request thing again, which could raise some questions.

Seeing Who Your Friends Are

If you can't recall who you've friended or need to access a friend's Profile page and you don't see that friend's name or picture, you can pull up a list of your friends by heading to your Timeline and clicking **See All** in your Friends box, near the top of your Timeline.

Check out who your friends are.

FRIEND-LY ADVICE

If you have lots of friends, you can narrow the list. Click the magnifying glass icon next to the search box at the top of the list and choose the desired option: **Search by Friends of**, **Search by Current City**, **Search by School**, **Search by Workplace**, **Search by Hometown**, or **Search by Interest**. Click in the text box next to the button and type the name of the friend, city, hometown, school, workplace, or interest, and press **Enter**.

Creating and Managing Friend Lists

If you're like most people, you have multiple social circles—family members, grade school classmates, high school classmates, co-workers and colleagues, and perhaps even members of your reading club. Unfortunately, your News Feed shows a mish-mash of all your friends' posts and updates, making the task of sorting out communications within each social circle nearly impossible.

Facebook's Friend List feature can make your social circles more manageable by assigning your friends to individual lists. After creating a friend list, you can use it to do the following:

- When viewing your News Feed (see Chapter 5), click a friend list to hide posts from everyone except the friends on the selected list.

- Send an email message to everyone on the friend list without having to address it to each and every individual. (See Chapter 6 for more about Facebook's Messages feature.)

- Make yourself available for chat with everyone on a friend list while hiding from everyone else.

- Post content that's shared with or hidden from people on a certain friend list.

- Send an event announcement and invitation to everyone on the friend list without having to address it to each and every individual. (See Chapter 11.)

- Tighten or loosen restrictions on your Timeline for different friend lists. (See Chapter 2 for more about Facebook privacy settings.)

Facebook supports three types of friend lists:

- **Default lists:** Facebook starts you out with three default friend lists: Close Friends, Acquaintances, and Restricted. People on the Restricted list can see only public posts and posts in which you've tagged them.

- **Smart lists:** Facebook creates a smart friend list for every network you claim you belong to: each school you've attended, each place you've worked, your hometown, the town where you currently live, and so on. Whenever one of your Facebook friends meets the criteria for inclusion on one of these lists, for example by reporting to have attended the same high school as you, that person is added to the list automatically.

- **Custom lists:** You can create your own friend lists, as explained in the next section.

To add a friend to an existing list, head to the friend's Timeline, mouse over the **Friends** button, and click the list you want to add the person to. If you don't see the list, click **Show All Lists**. When you add or remove friends, Facebook does so without notifying them.

Add a friend to an existing friend list.

Creating a Friend List

To create a friend list and add some friends to it, here's what you do:

1. Click **Home** (in the blue bar at the top).

2. Click **Friends**, in the left column. (If you don't see Friends, click the **More** button near the bottom of the column and then click **Friends**.)

3. Near the top of the center column, click **+ Create List**. The Create New List dialog box appears.

4. Click in the **List name** box and type a name for the list, such as Co-Workers, Family, or People I Used to Date.

5. Click in the **Members** box, start typing the name of a friend you want to add to the list, and then click the person's name. If you add a person by mistake, click the **X** next to the person's name to remove her.

6. Click **Create**. Facebook creates the list and displays it in the left menu, under Friends.

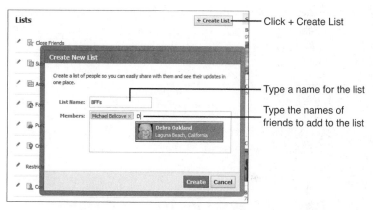

You can create a friend list and assign friends to it.

Managing a Friend List

You can manage a list by renaming it, adding or removing friends, changing criteria for inclusion on the list, and changing what list members are allowed to see. To configure a friend list, click **Home,** click **Friends** (in the left column), click the list you want to configure, click **Manage List** (upper-right corner), and click the type of change you want to make:

- **Rename List:** Displays a text box into which you can type a new name for the list.

- **Edit List:** Displays a screen you can use to add or remove friends from the list.

- **Choose Update Types:** Lets you choose the type of content to share with the friends on this list, including status updates, photos, game activity, comments, likes, and other activity.
- **Delete List:** Removes the list.

> **POKE**
>
> Certain friend lists might have additional items you can change; for example, the Manage List menu for your current town has an Edit Radius option, so you can increase the radius to include more friends or decrease the radius to include fewer friends in that list.

You can configure your friend lists.

Putting a Friend List to Good Use

Friend lists come in handy throughout Facebook, wherever and whenever you need to restrict or filter information from a select group of friends. In your News Feed, for example, you can click a friend list in the left column to filter out all posts except those from friends on the selected list. When you post content to your News Feed or Timeline, you can click the privacy button and choose a friend list to share the post with only the people on that list. You can also use friend lists when entering your privacy preferences, as discussed in Chapter 2, and configuring your About page, as explained in Chapter 3.

News Feed shows posts only from friends on the selected list

Click a friend List

Restrict and filter information with friend lists.

Deleting a Friend List

You can delete only the lists you've created. To delete a list, click **Home,** click **Friends** (in the left column), click the list you created, click **Manage List** (upper-right), and click **Delete List**. Facebook displays a dialog box warning that deleting the list isn't reversible and asking for your confirmation. Click **Delete List** to confirm or **Cancel** to abort the operation.

POKE

Although deleting a list is irreversible, it doesn't permanently remove your friends, so you can always re-create the list—assuming you remember who was on it.

You can't delete smart lists or default lists (Close Friends, Acquaintances, and Restricted), but you can disable them. To disable a smart list, click **Home** (blue bar at the top) and then **Friends** (in the left column), click the smart list you want to disable, click **Manage List** (upper-right), and click **Archive List**. To enable an archived list, repeat the steps but click **Restore List** instead of Archive List.

To disable a default list, just stop using it, and it'll eventually disappear from your Home page.

Expanding Your Reach with Networks

A Facebook network is a closed community for a workplace or school that enables members of that community to network in a more private environment. The network enables everyone in it to track down one another more easily and relax restrictions on what they want to share only with members of that network. Facebook allows you to join up to five different networks.

WHOA!

All members of a network must have an authenticated email address for that community; for example, if you want to join the Purdue University network, you need a Purdue University–approved email address that ends in something like @purdue.edu. Facebook must validate the email address before granting you access to the network.

To join a network, here's what you do:

1. Open the Account menu at the top right corner of any Facebook page and click **Account Settings**. The Account Settings page appears.

2. Click **Edit** next to Networks.

3. Click **Join a network**, click in the **Type a name** box, and start typing the name of your workplace, city, state, high school, or college. As you type, Facebook displays networks that match what you've typed so far.

4. Click the name of the network you want to join.

5. Click in the **Network email** text box and type the email address you have on that network.

6. Click **Save Changes**. Facebook updates the Networks page to show that you're now an active member of the network you just joined.

Joining a network makes your Profile accessible to network members, regardless of whether they're Facebook friends, so you might want to adjust your privacy settings for networks, as explained in Chapter 2.

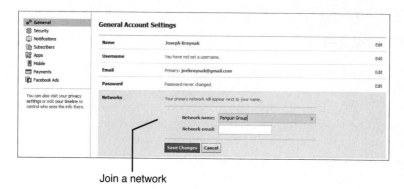

Join a network

You can join one or more networks to use Facebook in a sequestered community.

If you join only one network, it becomes your primary network. Whenever you perform a search, results from that network appear first in the search results. If you join two or more networks, only one can be your primary network. To change your primary network, open your **Account Settings** page, click **Edit** next to Networks, choose your primary network, and click **Save Changes**.

You can leave a network at any time. Open the **Account** menu (top-right corner), click **Account Settings**, click **Edit** next to Networks, click **Remove** next to the network you want to leave, and click **Save Changes**.

Introducing Your Friends

If you think two of your friends might enjoy knowing one another, consider introducing them. To introduce friends, head to the Timeline of the person to whom you want to introduce one or more of your friends and click **Suggest Friends** button. (If the button doesn't appear, it means your friend is not accepting friend suggestions.) The Suggest Friends for <Name> dialog box appears, prompting you to select some friends. Click each friend you want to introduce to this person, and then click the **Send Suggestions** button.

Click Suggest Friends

Introduce your friends to one another.

The Least You Need to Know

- Be selective when friending people on Facebook. Friends can view and access each other's status updates, Timelines, and other content.
- To search for someone on Facebook, click in the **Search** box (top menu), type the person's email address or name, and press **Enter**.
- To find more friends on Facebook, click **Find Friends** in the blue bar at the top, and use the resulting options to track down people you may know.
- When you receive a friend request, you have two options: Confirm and Not Now.
- Use friend lists to group friends and reduce some of the clutter in your News Feed.
- To dump a friend, head to the friend's Timeline, click the **Friends** button, and click **Unfriend**.

News Feeds, Timelines, and Tickers

In This Chapter

- Understanding the difference between your Timeline and News Feed
- Creating and posting status updates
- Commenting on friends' status updates
- Posting messages on friends' Timelines
- Communicating one-on-one via friendships
- Tracking your friends' activities in real time via the Ticker

Facebook provides three major modes of communication between and among friends—the News Feed, Timeline (or Wall, if you haven't yet switched to the Timeline), and Ticker. Your News Feed greets you whenever you log on. It's the column in the middle of the screen that asks, "What's on your mind?" and displays recent status updates that you and your friends have posted, along with other information—such as when a friend updates his relationship status or answers a question. If you wander away from your News Feed, you can always return to it by clicking **Home** or **facebook** in the top menu.

Your Timeline, on the other hand, is a more intimate place that displays only your posts and anything your friends have specifically posted to your Timeline. You can view your Timeline at any time by clicking your name or profile picture (in the top menu or at the top of the left-hand column).

When you click a friend's name, you're taken to that friend's Timeline page, where you can read her posts and post messages to this particular friend. As you reply to one another's Timeline posts, you engage in a friendship discussion that appears on both your Timelines.

If you're a frequent Facebook user, you have a Ticker, which enables you to keep up with the latest news as it happens, listen to music with friends, and engage in ongoing conversations.

In the following sections, you get a better feel for your News Feed, Timeline, and Ticker.

Homing In on Your News Feed

You can't miss your News Feed. Log on to Facebook, and it's right there, in your face, front and center. To filter out some of the "noise" and focus on the most important news of the day, Facebook's default setting for the News Feed is Top News. Facebook hides most of the status updates, displaying only the most important ones. To deem what's most important, Facebook considers numerous factors, including the number of friends commenting on a certain post, how often you seem to interact with each friend, and the type of content (photo, video, status update, or link).

To view every single status update from every one of your friends, which can get pretty cluttered and difficult to follow, click **Sort** (near the top of your News Feed) and then **Most Recent**.

Filtering Content

As your community of friends grows, assuming they're fairly active on Facebook, that News Feed can become very cluttered, even when you're viewing only the top news. The information you really want to see can easily get buried in a barrage of status updates, photos, videos, links, and events.

You can view all posts listed from newest to oldest or focus on the Top News.

Fortunately, you can select the type of content you want to view by clicking the desired option in the left menu. Click any of the following options to reduce the clutter:

- **News Feed:** This is your ticket back to the News Feed, just in case you wandered off and want to return.

- **Photos:** To display only the photos your friends have posted.

- **A friend list:** To display only content shared by your friends who are on the selected friend list.

Hiding a Friend's Updates

When a friend is monopolizing the conversation on your Timeline or News Feed by posting too much content that doesn't really interest you, you can easily hide that person's posts. To hide someone's posts, rest the mouse pointer on a post from the friend whose updates you want to hide, click the **∨** in the upper-right corner of the post, and choose the desired option:

- **Hide story:** Hides only this item.
- **Report story or spam:** Reports the item to Facebook as a violation.
- **Subscribed to <Name>:** Enables you to choose the relative number of items you want to see from this person in your News Feed: All Updates, Most Updates, or Only Important updates.
- **Unsubscribe from <Name>:** Unsubscribes you from the friend so nothing he or she posts appears in your News Feed.
- **Unsubscribe from blank by <Name>:** Unsubscribes you from only this type of content. For example, if this is a status update, the option is **Unsubscribe from status updates by <Name>**. If this is an activity update, the option is **Unsubscribe from activity stories by <Name>**.

You can hide a friend's updates.

You can unhide posts and content you've chosen to hide. To show a single post you've hidden, click **Undo** next to the post, if the Undo option is available. To show all posts from someone you've unsubscribed from, click **Undo** next to the post from the person you unsubscribed from. Facebook refreshes your News Feed to display the previously hidden posts.

Checking Out the Timeline or Wall

Facebook's Timeline or Wall is a more personal place for sharing with friends. Here, you and your friends can post status updates, photos, video clips, and life events that don't get swept away in the frenetic flow of the News Feed.

Every Facebook user has a Timeline or Wall, not both. Facebook is in the process of transitioning all Facebook users to the Timeline user interface, but not all users have made the transition, so you might still encounter the Wall, which looks a lot like the News Feed. Throughout this chapter, we focus on the Timeline. (For more about the differences between the Timeline and Wall, see Chapter 3.)

To access your Timeline, click your name or photo in the top menu or near the top of the left column.

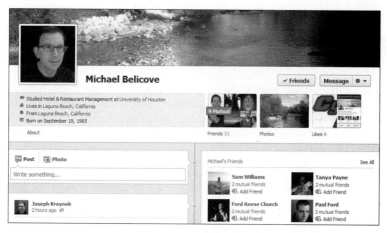

The Timeline records a member's history on Facebook and facilitates friend-to-friend interactions.

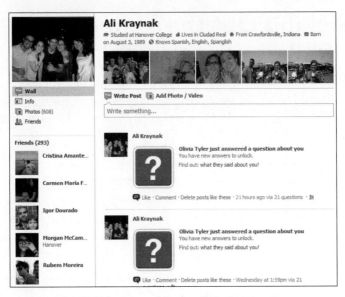

The Wall facilitates friend-to-friend interactions.

WHOA!

Communicating via Timelines reduces the frenetic clutter of status updates characteristic of the News Feed, but friendship discussions are not private. Anyone who can access your Timeline or your friend's Timeline can read the content of your posts, and some Timeline posts might show up in your mutual friends' News Feeds. You can restrict access to your Timeline by adjusting your privacy settings, as discussed in Chapter 2.

In the following sections, you find out how to access your Timeline and your friends' Timelines, configure your Timeline, and use Timelines to carry on more direct conversations with a friend.

Bumping Into a Friend's Timeline

Except for the content posted on a friend's Timeline, it looks almost identical to your own Timeline and contains many of the same features. Another difference is that your friend's Timeline has several buttons you can click to manage your friendship, subscribe or unsubscribe from specific content, send a message, and more.

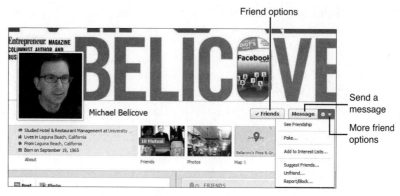

A friend's Timeline has a few special options.

Posting to Your Timeline or News Feed

At the top of the News Feed and the Timeline is Facebook's Publisher. Its primary purpose is to enable you to post text informing your friends of what you're doing, planning to do, thinking, or feeling at this very moment. It's very similar to posting a "tweet" on Twitter.com—something referred to as *microblogging*. You use the Publisher to post status updates (also called stories) and other content to your News Feed or Timeline or to a friend's Timeline.

Adding a post to your News Feed or Timeline is one of the easiest things to do on Facebook; follow these steps:

1. Click **Home** or **facebook** (in the top menu) to post in your News Feed or click your name or profile picture in the top menu or near the top of the left column to post to your Timeline. Either way, what you post will appear in both your News Feed and on your Timeline. (Click a friend to post the update to your friend's Timeline, addressing the post more directly to this particular friend.)

2. Click in the **What's on your mind?** box and type your message.

3. (Optional) Click any of the controls above the What's on your mind? box to post special content, as explained in the following sections.

4. (Optional) Click the privacy button (the button with "Friends" on it below and toward the right of where you typed your message) and click the desired privacy option:

   - **Public:** All Facebook members can read your post.
   - **Friends:** Only your Facebook friends can read the post. (This is the default setting.)
   - **Only Me:** Only you can see it.
   - **Custom:** Displays the Custom Privacy dialog box that provides additional control over who can read your post. If you have one or more friend lists, this comes in very handy for sharing a post with a select group of friends.
   - **A friend list:** You can choose a friend list, as explained in Chapter 4, to share the post with only those friends on the list.

5. Click **Share**. Facebook displays the update in the News Feed or on the Timeline where you posted it.

Post a status update to keep your friends informed about what you're up to.

You can always delete a post. Mouse over the posted item, click the **X** that appears in its upper-right corner, and click **Delete Post**. In the confirmation dialog box that appears, click **Delete Post**.

Asking a Question

A great way to solicit feedback from friends is to post a question. Facebook enables you to post only the question or post the question along with poll options to keep a running tally of what your friends think, such as whether you should change careers, start dating a certain someone, or which movie you should rent.

WHOA!

Don't ask a question you don't want people other than your Facebook friends to read it. When you post a question, your friends might share the question with their friends, who might share it with their friends, and so on. This can be a good thing if you want lots of feedback, but a bad thing if you didn't plan on sharing it with the world.

To post a question, click **Ask Question** near the What's on your mind? box and the box changes to Ask something …. Click in that box and type your question. If you want to poll your friends, click the **Add Poll Options** link and type your options in the resulting text boxes. To restrict the choices to the items you typed, deselect the option **Allow anyone to add options**. When you're ready to post the question, click **Post**.

Ask a question or poll Facebook members.

To see answers to a question you posted, click **facebook** or **Home** in the top menu, and then click **Questions** in the left-hand column.

Attaching a Photo or Video

Most people love viewing photos and videos, particularly interesting photos and footage of people they know and love, so consider including an occasional photo or video in your status updates. All you need to do is click the Publisher's **Add Photo/Video** link and follow the on-screen cues to upload the photo or video or use your webcam to take a photo. When you click **Add Photo/Video**, Facebook presents the following options:

- **Upload Photo/Video:** Click **Upload a Photo/Video**, click **Choose File**, select a photo stored on your computer, click **Open**, and Facebook uploads the photo or video for you.

- **Use Webcam:** Assuming your computer is equipped with a functioning webcam, click **Use Webcam**, give your permission to access the camera if prompted, close the prompt, and click the red and white record button to start recording. If you don't like the video, click the **X** in the upper-right corner and do a reshoot. If you're satisfied with the video, click **Post**.

- **Create Photo Album:** Click **Create Photo Album** and follow the on-screen instructions to upload photos and create your album.

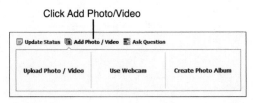

Click Add Photo/Video

Facebook prompts you to upload a photo or video, record a video with your webcam, or create a new photo album.

FRIEND-LY ADVICE

You can upload photos and videos by emailing them to your personalized upload email address. Log in to Facebook and go to **m.facebook.com/upload.php** to find your personal publishing email address. Type a description of the photos or videos you're uploading in the Subject line to include as a caption. Any photos or video you upload via email are public, but you can change the privacy setting for anything you upload later. If you send an email message without attachments, whatever you type in the Subject line becomes a status update.

Inserting a Link

To call attention to web content outside your News Feed, you can easily post a link to it. Your friends can then click the link to check out the web page for themselves.

Before you share a link, make sure you have the right address of the page you want to link to. Open that page in your browser window, click in the **Address** box to highlight the page's address, and then press the keystroke you use to copy stuff. (You may be able to right-click the link and click **Copy**.) You can now share the link.

Right-click in the **What's on your mind?** box and click **Paste**. Facebook downloads the title and description of the page along with any small images that appear on the page. Use the arrow buttons to select the thumbnail you want, or click **No Thumbnail**. Type something in the text box if you want to say something about the link (you can delete the link address at this point, if desired), and then click **Post**.

Type or paste a web page address

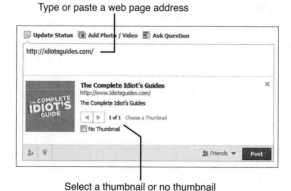

Select a thumbnail or no thumbnail

You can link to web pages from the Publisher.

Responding to a Friend's Post

When a friend posts something to his Timeline or it shows up in your News Feed, you can then read the update, post a comment on it, "like" it (give it the thumbs up), and even share it with your other friends. If you don't see a friend's posts in your News Feed, then head to the person's Timeline, where you can read and comment on the friend's posts there.

Posting a Comment

You can respond to a friend's post by commenting on it. Click in the **Write a comment …** box just below the message, type your comment, and press **Enter** to post your comment. (If the Write a comment… box isn't visible, you might need to click the **Comment** link that appears near your friend's status update.)

WHOA!

Whatever you write as a comment will be viewable by all of your friend's Facebook friends as well as all your friends. If your comment is of a highly personal nature, take a minute to think it through before commenting in public, and consider sending your thoughts with a Facebook Message instead. See Chapter 6 for more about Facebook's Message feature.

Click Comment

Type your comment and press Enter

You can easily comment on a friend's post.

Liking and Sharing a Post

Even easier than posting a comment is to express your approval of what your friend posted. All you need to do is click the **Like** link just below the post. A little thumbs-up icon appears, along with your username, indicating your vote of approval.

Another way to respond to a friend's post is to share it with your friends by posting it to your News Feed or sending it via a message to one or more friends. Click the **Share** link below the post. (The Share link appears only if your friend's privacy settings allow friends to share.) Open the **Share** menu in the upper-left corner of the Share dialog box that displays, and choose to share the item on your Timeline, a friend's Timeline, in a group, on a page, or in a private message. Address the message to the friend, group, page, or whatever you selected from the Share menu, click in the **Write Something ...** box, type a brief message introducing the item you're reposting and indicating why you think it's noteworthy, and click the **Share** button.

Posting to a Friend's Timeline

Assuming your friend allows friends to post to her Timeline and hasn't specifically blocked you from doing so, you can write on your friend's Timeline by posting a message or comment. Whatever you post can be seen not only by your friend but also by any of your friend's friends. It will also appear in your mutual friends' News Feeds.

To post to your friend's Timeline, first head there by clicking your friend's name or photo. You can then proceed to do one of the following:

- Click in the **Write something ...** box, type your message, attach something if you like, and click **Share**.
- Click the **Comment** link below any of your friend's posts, type a comment, and press **Enter**.

Connecting One-on-One via a Friendship Page

As the old saying goes, "Two's company; three's a crowd." Fortunately, Facebook enables you to focus on your one-to-one relationships free of the usual clutter on your Timeline or News Feed. To see a friendship, head to a friend's Timeline, click the button to the right of the Message button, and click **See Friendship**.

Check out a friendship.

This takes you to your friendship page with this particular friend, where you can engage in one-on-one discussions. Everything your friend posts on your Timeline, including comments to your posts, appears on this friendship page that the two of you can access. This doesn't mean, however, that your conversations between one another are necessarily private. Your other friends may be able to check out the conversations depending on your privacy settings.

Your friendship page gives you a virtual snapshot of your Facebook friendship, displaying Timeline posts you've exchanged, mutual friends, events you've both attended, photos you're both tagged in, and things you both "like."

If the discussion doesn't include you, you can still comment on or "like" one of your friend's status updates, but you can't post a comment of your own. If you're involved in the discussion, you can post a comment or a follow-up post, which then appears on the friendship page.

You can follow discussions between friends.

Wishing a Friend a Happy Birthday

Most people, unless they're hard-core curmudgeons or would rather be dead, appreciate receiving a birthday note, so if a friend's birthday is coming up, consider wishing him a happy birthday on Facebook. Facebook will even remind you! Even though it has hundreds of million of users, Facebook does a spectacular job of keeping track of everyone's birthday. In the column to the right of your News Feed, Facebook displays reminders of any of your friends' birthdays that are coming up soon.

To receive advance notification of upcoming friends' birthdays via email, open the **Account** menu (top-right corner), click **Account Settings**, click the **Notifications** tab, click **Edit** next to Facebook, click the check box next to **Has a birthday coming up (weekly message)**, and click the **Save Changes** button. Each week you'll receive a concise email from Facebook with information about your friends' upcoming birthdays.

Poking a Friend

On Facebook, you can poke or be poked. When you poke a friend, you're letting the person know you're thinking of her. She can then poke you back or simply ignore you.

To poke a friend, head to the person's Timeline by clicking on her name or Profile image, click the button to the right of the Message button, and click **Poke**. This sends a Poke notification to your friend's Home page with the options to Poke Back or click the **X** next to the poke to remove it.

If someone is poking you incessantly and won't stop even after you ask him to, you can block the person, as explained in Chapter 2. You can disable poking notifications that show up in your email Inbox on the Notifications tab in Account Settings.

Liking and Sharing Stuff

Sprinkled throughout Facebook and all over the web are links that enable you to share content with your friends on Facebook or "like" it:

- **Like:** When you click **Like**, Facebook immediately posts a link to the content to your Timeline and News Feed.
- **Share:** When you click **Share**, Facebook displays a dialog box that enables you to choose how to share the item (by posting it or sending it as a message to select friends) and add a description of the item or a brief explanation of why you think your friends will find it relevant.

From within Facebook, you can share or Like your friends' status updates, photos, videos, notes, and anything else containing the Share or Like option. You're likely to see the Facebook Share or Like option in all sorts of places—on news websites, web pages, blog posts, photo sites, video sites, and so on.

On some sites, you might see a different type of share icon that doesn't look like the Facebook Like or Share link, but it still enables you to share on Facebook. If you see a generic share icon, try clicking it. It may open a menu that provides options for sharing the content on Facebook, Twitter, MySpace, and other social networks. You can proceed by clicking the option to share the item on Facebook.

Click Like

> *The Facebook Like option is popping up on sites
> all over the web.*

After you click the option to share on Facebook, you're automatically transported to Facebook where you can log in (if you're not already logged in) and complete the Post to Profile box. Type a message introducing the content you're about to share, and then click the **Post** button.

WHOA!

Share with care. You can seriously damage or destroy a relationship by sharing content that a friend strongly disagrees with, finds offensive, or had no intention of sharing with others. When choosing material to share, consider avoiding hot-button issues like politics or religion. And never, ever pass along sensitive information that your friend shared with you in confidence. If you have any doubt about sharing something a friend posted, ask your friend before sharing it with others.

Choose where to share

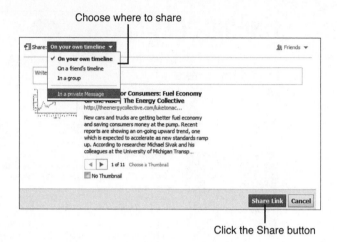

Click the Share button

*You can share a friend's post by posting it to your
Timeline and News Feed.*

Sharing More Substantial Content via Notes

In the world of Facebook, you use notes instead of status updates when you have a lot to say or want more control over its appearance. Although status updates are exclusively of the plain-text variety, you can format a Note using HTML (hypertext markup language) tags, such as <bold> for bold, <i> for italics, and <u> for an underline. In other words, you can get a little fancier with your formatting.

Posting a Note

To post a Note, click **facebook** at the top left of any page, followed by **Apps** (left column) to expand your Apps list, click **Notes**, and then click the **+ Write a Note** button to the right of Notes at the top of the middle column. The Write a Note page appears. Click in the **Title** box and type a brief, descriptive, and compelling title for your note (otherwise, nobody will want to read it). Click in the **Body** box and type whatever you want to say.

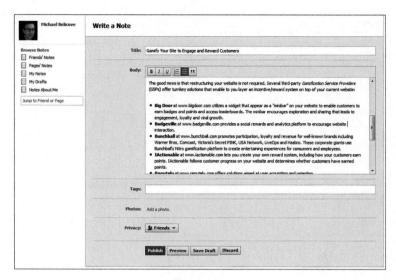

Post a note.

You can format the text using the formatting buttons in the Body toolbar or by typing HTML tags, as presented in Table 5.1.

Table 5.1 HTML Tags for Formatting Notes

Format	HTML Tag Example Use
Bold	\Bold\
Italics	\<i>Italics\</i>
<u>Underline</u>	\<u>Underline\</u>
~~Strikethrough~~	\<s>Strikethrough\</s>
Big size	\<big>Big size\</big>
Small size	\<small>Small size\</small>
Em dash like —	\—
Hyperlink to IdiotsGuides.com	\<a href="http://idiotsguides.com/">IdiotsGuides.com\</a>
Bulleted (Unordered) list • Item • Item • Item • Item	\<ul> \<li>Item\</li> \<li>Item\</li> \<li>Item\</li> \<li>Item\</li> \</ul>

continues

Format	HTML Tag Example Use
Numbered (Ordered) List 1. Step one 2. Step two 3. Step three 4. Step four	<ol> <li>Step one</li> <li>Step two</li> <li>Step three</li> <li>Step four</li> </ol>
Indented quote	<blockquote>Indented quote </blockquote>
# Heading 1	<h1>Heading 1</h1>
## Heading 2	<h2>Heading 2</h2>
### Heading 3	<h3>Heading 3</h3>

POKE

HTML tags come in two flavors—paired and unpaired. For paired tags, you type a tag where you want the element to begin and another tag where you want it to end; for example, <i>italics</i> displays *italics*. Unpaired codes stand alone, such as &mdash, which inserts an em dash that looks like this: —.

After composing your note, you can tag Facebook friends mentioned in the note or friends you want to make sure know about the note. To tag a friend, click in the **Tags** box, start typing your friend's name, and, when you see the name of the friend you want to tag, click it. Repeat the steps to tag other friends. After you post the note, Facebook automatically places a message on tagged friends' News Feed about the existence of your note and sends them notifications (assuming they didn't disable notifications for notes).

Below the Body box are options to **Add a photo** (to upload a new photo or import a photo you previously uploaded). No surprises here, but if you need a refresher course on working with photos in Facebook, check out Chapter 7. Another option is to use the HTML <img> tag to insert the image, but you have to know the online address of the image and its filename; for example, <img src="http://idiotsguides.com/img.jpg" />

Below the **Add a photo** option, you find the **Privacy** settings. Open the **Privacy** list and select the option that best represents the Facebook members you want to be able to access your note: **Public**, **Friends**, **Only Me**, or **Customize**. The Customize option enables you to cherry-pick individuals who can see the note; for example, a specific Facebook friend or only those friends on a particular friend list.

When you're done composing your note and entering your privacy preferences, you have several options on how to proceed. Prior to publishing your post, we recommend that you click **Preview**, especially if you used any HTML tags to format your text. If everything looks fine, then you can publish it. If not, you can choose the option to edit the post. You also have the option to Save Draft (so you can complete the note and publish it later) or Discard to delete the note. When you're ready to publish it, click the **Publish** button.

Discovering More About Notes

The Notes app does more than enable you to post notes. When you go to your Home page and click **Notes**, in the left column, your Notes page appears, displaying all of the notes you've posted either to your Timeline or a page you've created (see Chapter 16 for more about pages), notes your Facebook friends have posted, notes in which you've been tagged, and any note drafts you've saved. You can filter the contents of your Notes page by selecting the desired option below Notes, in the left column: **Page's Notes**, **My Drafts**, **Notes About Me**, or **My Notes**.

In addition, a thumbnail for the Notes app appears in your and your Facebook friends' Timelines. Click the Notes thumbnail in your Timeline to view your notes, notes about you, and the + Write a Note button for posting a new note to your Timeline. If you go to a Facebook friend's Timeline, and the friend uses Notes, click the Notes thumbnail to view notes that your friend has posted and notes about your friend. You can post a comment to a friend's note. (If you don't see a Notes thumbnail, try clicking the down arrow button to the right of the thumbnails to expand the thumbnails area. If you still don't see a Notes thumbnail, your friend might not be using Notes or might have deleted the thumbnail.)

Interacting in Real Time with the Ticker

If you have a lot of friends on Facebook, interact with them frequently, and use Facebook apps, you probably have the Facebook Ticker in the right column of your Home page. The Ticker displays updates in real time, letting you know what your Facebook friends are up to as they post content and engage in activities on Facebook, such as listening to music, watching video clips, or discussing the latest news.

The cool thing about the Ticker is that it enables you to engage and interact with your friends in real time. Hover over an item in the Ticker to display a pop-up box with available options, which vary depending on the selected item. For example, if a friend is listening to a particular tune, you can choose to listen to the same tune. If you don't have the Facebook app required to listen to the tune, you can click a link to get the app.

If you have the Ticker, you can go online to chat and have the Ticker bar appear above the list of friends on your chat list. To change the relative lengths of the two lists, drag the bar that separates them. To return the Ticker to its original location, mouse over the lower right corner of the sidebar and click the **Hide Sidebar** button.

The Least You Need to Know

- Your News Feed contains a running account of status updates that you and your friends post on Facebook, whereas your Timeline contains information about you and your personal interactions on Facebook.

- Posting a status update is easy. Click **What's on your mind?** in the Publisher, type a message, and click **Post**.

- You can post photos and videos by clicking on the appropriate icon in the Publisher.

- To comment on a friend's post, click the **Comment** link below the post or click in the **Write a comment** box, type your comment, and press **Enter**.

- To share or "like" content on or outside of Facebook, click the Facebook **Share** or **Like** icon or link: Like posts the content immediately to your News Feed and Timeline, whereas Share displays a dialog box, so you can add some commentary or share it via a message.

- Use the Ticker to engage with friends in real time.

Communicating via Messages and Chat

In This Chapter

- Reading incoming messages
- Sending messages to friends and strangers
- Engaging in conversations with one or more friends
- Adding and removing people from ongoing conversations
- Chatting via text, voice, and video

Although most of Facebook is focused on some degree of public sharing, several features enable you to communicate in private with one or more Facebook friends, including messages, chats, texts, and email (assuming you choose to create an @facebook. com email address). This enables you to pull up a conversation with someone and view a complete history of your interactions on and off Facebook. You can even loop new people into a conversation and leave a conversation that no longer interests you. This chapter shows you how.

Activating Email, Texting, Chat, and Video Calling

Head to your Home page and click **Messages** (in the left menu). Regardless of whether you have any messages, you should see a bar just above the Messages area that includes four steps to fully access Facebook's Messages feature. (If the bar isn't displayed, these features may have already been set up.) You don't need to perform all four steps. Activate only the features you want to use.

- **Claim your Facebook email:** You can claim your Facebook email address of yourname@facebook.com so Facebook can help you track your email exchanges that occur outside the confines of Facebook. To activate Facebook email, click **Claim your Facebook email**, use the resulting box to choose your email address, and click **Activate Email**.

- **Turn on text messaging:** To enable your Facebook friends to send text messages to your mobile device, click **Turn on text messaging**, use the resulting box to choose your country and mobile carrier, click **Next**, and follow the on-screen cues to complete the operation. (See Chapter 15 for more about Facebook Mobile.)

- **Chat is online / Go online to chat:** If you chose to go offline with Facebook Chat, you can click **Go online to chat** so your friends can converse with you via Chat and Facebook can log your conversations as messages.

- **Video calling:** This option should show that video calling is set up, but if it's not, click the option and follow the on-screen prompts to enable video calling.

Activate the features you want to use.

Accessing Messages

Whenever you log in to Facebook, the top menu shows the number of messages you've received but haven't yet read (if any). To view a list of recent messages, click the **Messages** icon. The Messages menu drops down, displaying several of your most recent messages with the newest message first. (If you have no new messages, the Messages icon is barely visible.)

To get to your Messages page, click **See All Messages** (at the bottom of the menu) or, from your Home page, click **Messages** (left menu). This takes you to a list of all messages you received—both those you have and haven't read. Unread messages are shaded a light blue and have a dark blue dot next to them; those you've already read are unshaded with a circle next to them.

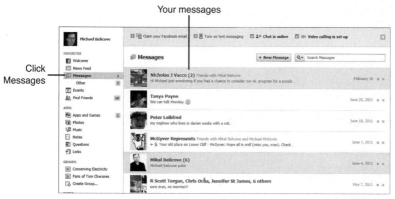

Your Messages area displays a list of messages you received.

Reading and Replying to New Messages

To read a message, click it. Facebook displays all messages you've exchanged with this person along with a record of when you called one another. Click in the **Write a reply...** text box below the message, type your message, and click **Reply**. In addition to replying with text, you can attach a file, photo, or video by clicking the relevant icon below the text box.

Below and to the right of the Write a reply box is a check box that toggles Quick Reply mode. When Quick Reply is on, you type your message and press **Enter** to send it. When Quick Reply is off, you type your message and then click the **Reply** or **Reply All** button to send it. (If Quick Reply is off, pressing **Enter** starts a new paragraph.) You might also see an option that enables you to send a copy of the reply to the person's mobile phone.

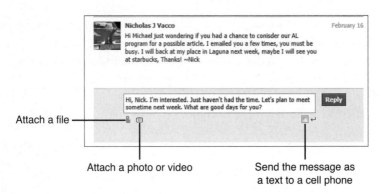

Attach a file

Attach a photo or video

Send the message as a text to a cell phone

The message appears and you can reply to it.

If you received a message and replied to it, or you sent a message and the recipient replied, both the original message and response are shown together; that way, you can follow the discussion thread without having to search for old messages to see what you or someone else said.

You can always return to the list of messages by clicking **Messages** in the left menu or the **< Messages** button above the conversation.

Forwarding a Message

You can forward one or more messages in a conversation or the entire conversation to another friend. First, open the conversation on its own page. Then, click **Actions** (upper right) **Forward**. Click each message you want to forward so a checkmark appears next to it, and then click **Forward**. The Forward Message box appears.

Click in the **To** box and start typing the future recipient's name or email address. As you start to type, Facebook displays the names of your Facebook friends that match what you've typed so far. If you see the desired name, click it. If not, keep typing. You can add more names and email addresses if you'd like to forward the message to additional recipients.

Click in the **Message** box, type an explanation of why you're forwarding the message, and then click the **Send** button.

Searching for Messages

Given that Facebook gathers messages from a variety of sources, you can expect your inbox to become quite cluttered. To help you sort through the mounds of messages, Facebook includes a search tool.

You can search for messages by name (sender or recipient) or by keyword (to find all messages that mention the upcoming family reunion, for example). To search for a message, click in the **Search Messages** box, type a friend's name or a keyword or phrase, and press **Enter**.

FRIEND-LY ADVICE

If you're typing a friend's name, you usually need to type only the first few letters. Facebook auto-completes the entry for you.

Facebook displays a list of all the messages that match your search entry. You can then click the message you want to read.

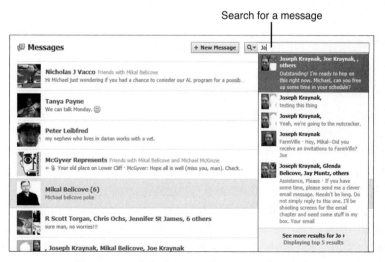

You can search for messages by name or keyword.

You can also filter the list of messages to show only Unread, Archived, or Sent messages or those you've sent and received using your Facebook email address. To filter messages, click the magnifying glass icon to the left of the Search Messages box and click the desired option: **Unread Messages**, **Archived Messages**, **Sent Messages**, or **Email Only**.

Flagging Messages as Unread

As you open messages, presumably to read them, Facebook marks them as "read." This means the message no longer appears in the count of new messages that Facebook displays next to the Messages icon in the top menu. It also means you can open the Search menu and click **Unread Messages** above the message list to display only those messages you've already read.

If a message is important, you might want to flag it as unread after reading it. To flag a single message as unread, click the circle (to the right of the message). The circle turns into a dot. To mark a message as read, click the dot to turn it into a circle. When you rest the mouse pointer on the circle or dot, Mark as Read or Mark as Unread appears, so you can tell whether you're about to mark the message as read or unread.

If you're viewing a message by itself (not in the list of messages), an Actions button appears above the message. To mark the message as unread, click **Actions** and then **Mark as Unread**.

Archiving or Deleting a Message

When you're done with a particular message or discussion, you can archive or delete it. If you're viewing a list of messages, you can only archive (not delete) messages from the list. (Archiving removes the message from the list but stores it in the archives so you can get it back later.) To archive a message, click the **X** (to the right of the last message we checked).

If you're viewing a message on its own page, you can archive or delete it. Click the **Actions** button (above and to the right of the conversation) and click the desired action: **Archive** or **Delete Messages**. If you choose to delete messages, a check box appears next to each message in the conversation. You can click the check box next to each message you want to delete and then click **Delete Selected** or click **Delete All** to delete the entire conversation.

> **WHOA!**
>
> Deleting a thread (discussion) deletes all messages in that discussion— so before you click that Delete button, make sure you really want everything in that thread deleted.

Reporting Spam

Facebook's setup is not prone to spam, but spammers are known to bend and break the rules. As a result, you might become the unfortunate recipient of Facebook email spam. If you do receive spam, report it to Facebook so management can crack down on the perpetrators.

To report spam, select the spam message or conversation, click the **Actions** button (above and to the right of the conversation), and click **Report as Spam**. The Report as Spam? dialog box appears prompting you for confirmation. Click **Report as Spam**.

Outgoing! Sending Messages

Usually, you have to send mail to get mail, so if you want a Messages list brimming with messages from your Facebook friends, start composing and sending messages. In the following sections, we show you how to compose a new message to send to an individual or to multiple recipients, whether the person is your Facebook friend or not.

Sending a New Message to a Facebook Member

Composing and sending a message in Facebook is a snap. Click the **Messages** icon in the top menu and click **Send a New Message** or, if the Messages screen is already displayed, click **+ New Message** (upper right). The New Message dialog box appears.

Now do the same thing you usually do when sending email: address the message in the To box, type a message in the Message box, and click **Send**. When addressing your message, instead of typing an email address, click in the **To** box and type a friend's name. (As you start typing, Facebook displays the names of friends that match what you typed so far. You can click a name to add it to the To box.)

Prior to sending the message, you can click the paperclip icon to attach a file or click the camera icon to take a photo or video of yourself (using your webcam) to attach to the outgoing message. You might also want to click the check box below and to the right of the Message box to text a copy of the message to the person's mobile device. (See Chapters 7 and 8 for more about pictures and video and Chapter 15 for more about Facebook Mobile.)

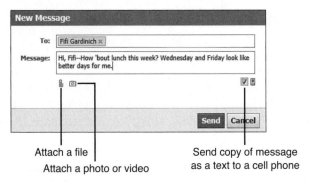

Send a message.

You can usually contact a person via Facebook messaging through the person's Timeline, even if the individual isn't a Facebook friend. To do so, go to the person's Timeline and click the **Message** button (upper right). Complete the message form and click **Send**.

POKE

If you're wondering where the Subject box is, Facebook has omitted it intentionally to make messages appear more conversational and less like traditional email. If someone sends you an email message that includes a subject line, the subject line appears in bold as the first line of the message.

Sending a Message to an Address Outside Facebook

You can send messages to email addresses outside Facebook, regardless of whether the recipient is a Facebook member, by typing the person's email address, instead of a friend's name, into the **To** box. Before you email outside Facebook, note the following:

- Non-Facebook members can receive your messages, but they can respond to your message only if you have a Facebook email address. Otherwise, to reply, they must click a link inside the message that opens a Facebook page and prompts the person to join Facebook.

- Don't spam from Facebook. If someone complains, Facebook might cancel your account.

Mass Mailing to Multiple Recipients

You can send the same message to several recipients with a single click of a button by entering a friend list or multiple friends' names and/or email addresses in the **To** box. (See Chapter 4 for instructions on how to create a friend list.)

WHOA!

Be careful when replying. Facebook members have been known to mistakenly send a reply to the entire group, thinking they were replying only to a particular individual. If the message contains something embarrassing or insulting to one or more group members you thought you were excluding, you could have a lot of explaining to do and apologies to make.

The tricky part is when you're carrying on an email discussion with multiple friends. If someone replies to your message and sends the reply to the entire group, you have the option of replying to the entire group or to that particular individual. Here's what you do:

- To reply to the group, type your message in the **Reply** box and click the **Reply** button.

- To reply to the individual only, click the person's name or email address, type your message in the **Reply** box, and click the **Reply** button. This creates a *branched thread* in which you and the other person can carry on a discussion outside the main discussion.

Chatting on Facebook

Chatting on Facebook is a snap. Assuming one of your friends is logged in and online (more about the online thing in a minute), here's what you do:

1. Click the thumbnail of the friend with whom you want to chat (left column, bottom). Or click **Chat** (lower-right corner of any Facebook page) and click the name of the friend with whom you want to chat. Either way, a chat box appears.

2. Type a message and press **Enter**. Your message pops up in the chat box on your screen and your friend's screen. Assuming your friend responds, his message pops up right below yours.

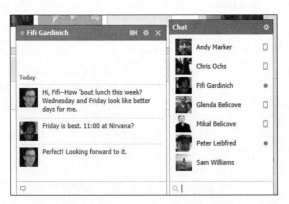

Chat on Facebook with your friends.

You can carry on Chat sessions with more than one friend at a time. Each Chat session appears in its own box with its own tab. To change from one Chat session to another, click the tab for the friend with whom you want to chat.

You can click the bar at the top of any chat window to make the window disappear without closing it. A tab for the window appears (typically the bottom right of the screen), and a red balloon icon appears to notify you whenever someone sends you a chat message. If your speakers are on and the volume's turned up, you'll also hear an audio cue whenever someone sends you a new message.

When you're ready to end a session and close the chat window, just click the **X** next to your friend's name.

If one of your friends sends you a message to start a Chat session, a chat window pops up, enabling you to reply.

Adding Someone to the Conversation

When you need to bring someone else into the loop, you can add the person to the conversation. Click the gear icon near the upper-right corner of the chat window and click **Add Friends to Chat**. Start typing the name of the friend you want to add and then click the name when it appears. You can repeat the step to add more friends to the conversation. Then click **Done**.

A new chat window appears, and its title bar includes the names of more people involved in the conversation. Whenever someone in the conversation posts a message, it appears in everyone's chat window.

Add someone to the conversation.

Leaving the Conversation

Whether you started the conversation or one of your friends included you in it, you can always leave. Click the gear icon near the upper-right corner of the chat window and click **Leave Conversation**.

Viewing Your Entire Conversation

When you're chatting with a friend, you're talking in real time and see only a small portion of your conversation. To see your entire conversation, including messages and chat, click the gear icon in the upper-right corner of the window in which you're chatting and click **See Full Conversation**. Facebook takes you to the Messages window, where you can view everything the two of you have said to one another over the entire course of your Facebook relationship.

To return to chat, click the **Actions** button, near the upper-right corner of the Messages page, and click **Open in Chat**.

If you're having a group conversation via the Messages window, the Actions menu contains several options that you normally don't see on the Actions menu when you're exchanging messages with only one other person, including Open in Chat, Add People, and Leave Conversation.

Viewing and Clearing Your Chat History

Facebook keeps a log of your chat history so you can pick up where you left off when you ended your last Chat session with a friend. When you begin a new Chat session, you can see the last few lines of your previous session.

You can clear the chat history at any time to prevent snoopy family members or officemates from nosing in on your business or just reduce the clutter of messages. Scroll to the top of the chat window and click **Clear Window**.

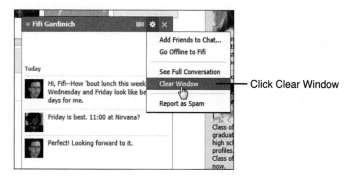

— Click Clear Window

Clear your chat history.

Clearing the chat history doesn't entirely remove the conversation. Facebook also stores your chats as messages, so you have an entire history of your correspondence with everyone via messages, chat, text messaging, and email. To view your messages, head to your Home page and click **Messages** (in the left menu). To view a conversation, click the most recent message from the person you were conversing with. You can then use options on the Actions menu to manage your messages, including the option to Delete Messages.

Going Online and Offline

Unless you tell Facebook otherwise, whenever you're logged in, you're online and ready to chat. If a friend opens his Chat menu, your name appears on that menu, and he can click it to start chatting with you. If you choose to go offline, you're invisible and friends can't tell you're online; however, they can send you a message that you can choose to respond to via Chat. To go offline or come back online, here's what you do:

- **Go offline:** Click **Chat**, click the gear icon to open the Options menu, and click **Go Offline**.
- **Go online:** Click **Chat**.

To appear online or offline to people on a certain friend list, click **Chat**, click the gear icon to open the Options menu, and click **Advanced Settings**. You can then choose to have all your friends see you except specific friends or those on the friend lists you specify, have only certain friends or friend lists see you, or have no one see you.

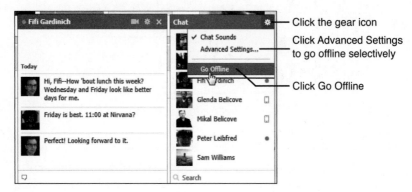

You can go offline to be incommunicado.

POKE

When you're engaged in a chat, you can go offline with only that friend. Click the gear icon in the chat window in which you're chatting and click **Go Offline to <Name>**. The chat window remains open with a link you can click to **Go Online to <Name>**. If you close that window and want to go back online to the friend, click the gear icon, **Advanced Settings**, and then the **x** next to the friend's name, and click **Save**.

Playing Chat Sounds

Assuming you have speakers or earphones plugged into your computer and they're turned on, whenever someone sends you a message, Facebook dings you. Actually, it sounds more like the popping noise you make when you smack your lips. You can toggle this option on or off; click **Chat > Options > Chat Sounds**.

Calling a Friend: Voice and Video Chat

Facebook has teamed up with Skype to offer video calls, so you can hear and see the person you're talking to, assuming you and your friend both have webcams connected to your computers. If either of you doesn't have a webcam, but your computers are equipped with a sound card, speakers, and a microphone, you can still call one another without the video component.

To start a video call, do one of the following:

- Head to your friend's Timeline, click the gear icon in the upper-right corner, and click **Call**. (You may see a Call button on the person's Timeline page, in which case you can click the Call button instead of having to select Call from the Options menu.)

- Click **Chat** (lower-right corner of any Facebook page) and click the name of the friend with whom you want to chat. The chat window appears. Click the video camera icon near the upper-right corner of the chat window.

If this is your first time using the video call feature, Facebook prompts you to install the Facebook Video Calling Plugin. Click the **Set Up** button and follow the on-screen prompts to complete the installation.

Click the video icon

Engage in video calls with your friends.

After you install the Facebook Video Calling Plugin, Facebook places the call. A dialog box appears on your friend's screen asking whether she wants to accept the call. Assuming she accepts, you can start talking. (If she hasn't completed the setup, you'll need to wait until she does.) You should see a window that streams live video of your friend, and your friend should see a window that streams live video of you.

If your friend is online but unavailable, Facebook prompts you to leave a recorded message. Click **Record Message** and follow the on-screen cues to record and send your message.

> **POKE**
>
> Voice and video chats are not recorded, but they are logged; that is, Facebook notes the date of each call and displays it in the running list of messages between you and your friend.

To end a video call, simply close the window.

Start talking.

The Least You Need to Know

- To access Facebook's messaging platform from your Home page, click **Messages** in the left menu or click the **Messages** icon (top menu) and then click **See All Messages**.

- To send a message, click the **Messages** icon (top menu) and then click **Send a New Message** or click the **+ New Message** button on the Messages screen and do the usual email thing.

- You can send messages to people who are not Facebook members by typing their email address into the **To** box.

- To strike up a conversation with a friend who's currently online, click **Chat** (bottom right) and then click the friend's name.

- To go offline and hide from friends who might want to chat with you, click **Chat**, click the gear icon, and click **Go Offline**.

- To voice or video chat with a friend, open a chat with the friend and click the video icon in the upper-right corner of the chat window.

Getting More Involved with Facebook

Although you establish and maintain relationships through Facebook, you also have a relationship with Facebook that develops over time as you get to know one another. The more Facebook knows about you and your friends, the better able it is to suggest new friends and present you with more relevant content. The more you know about Facebook, the better equipped you are to tap its full potential.

When you're ready to take your relationship with Facebook to the next level, we're ready to ramp you up. Here, we introduce you to one of the most popular features on Facebook—photo sharing—along with other features you may want to explore, including video sharing, groups, and events. We also provide a chapter specifically for parents, teachers, and other guardians of our youth in which we provide guidance on Facebook safety.

Uploading and Sharing Photos

In This Chapter

- Viewing other people's photos
- Making photo albums to organize your photos
- Uploading quality photos on Facebook
- Tagging yourself and your friends in photos
- Sharing photos selectively

Swapping photos online has become a favorite global pastime. With online photo-sharing services including Photobucket and Flickr, people can upload their photos and share them with anyone in the world who has a computer with internet access.

Well, Facebook is in the photo-sharing business, too. All you have to do is create a photo album, upload your photos, and start sharing. This chapter shows you how and provides additional guidance on restricting photo access to only those people you want looking at them.

Looking at Photos

Chances are pretty good that if you've spent more than two minutes on Facebook, you've already seen a few photos. They show up in the following places:

- **News Feed:** You can post photos to your News Feed, and if a friend posts a photo, a thumbnail version of it appears in your News Feed. You can click the photo to view a larger version and access any other photos in that album.

- **Timeline:** Depending on the privacy settings, you and your friends can post photos to each other's Timelines. In addition, you can click **Photos** in the cover area of a person's Timeline to access that person's photo albums.

- **Groups:** If you belong to any Facebook groups, as explained in Chapter 9, you can view photos that group members have posted.

- **Photo application:** On your Home page, in the left menu, click **Photos**. On the Photos page that appears you can view albums your friends have recently created or updated, photos uploaded using a mobile device, photos in which your friends have been tagged, your photos, and photos of you. Using the Photos application, you can also create your own albums, as explained in the following section.

Access Facebook's Photos app.

POKE

Neither Photobucket nor Flickr can claim the top spot in the online photo-sharing arena. Facebook is the champ with more than 3 billion photos uploaded to the site each month.

Preparing Photos for Uploading

After you've created an album, you can immediately begin uploading photos from your computer to the new album, but don't rush the process. First, make sure those photos are quality snapshots, and then organize them into folders on your computer to simplify the upload process. The following sections show you how to properly prepare your photos for upload.

Editing Your Photos: Quality Counts

Too many Facebook members focus, snap, and upload—often skimping on the "focus" part. As a result, their albums are cluttered with lousy snapshots—too dark, too light, too much glare, weird colors, out of focus, and so on. Prior to uploading your photos, use a photo-editing program to make them look as good as they possibly can be. You can't do much for those out-of-focus shots, but you can fix just about anything else.

Most digital cameras and many printers come with their own photo-editing software. If you have no such program on your computer, consider first uploading the photos to a photo-sharing service, such as Flickr (www.flickr.com), that has photo-editing tools. You can then import your photos into Facebook as explained later in this chapter. Google's Picasa (www.picasa.google.com) is another option. With Picasa, you edit the photos on your computer and then upload them to Picasa to share them. With a Picasa Facebook app, you can even upload your photos to Facebook right after editing them. We cover Flickr and Picasa near the end of this chapter.

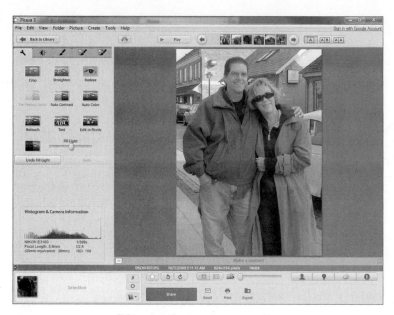

Edit your photos to ensure quality.

Organizing Photos into Folders

Whenever you *download* photos from your camera to your computer, you should store the photos in separate folders. Each folder can function as a separate album. This enables you to quickly upload an entire folder full of photos from your computer to one of your Facebook albums without having to select individual photos to include or exclude.

If you haven't organized the photos on your computer in separate folders, take some time and organize them now. We'll wait.

Uploading Photos

To make photos available on Facebook, you need to upload (copy) them from your computer or mobile device to Facebook. As with most tasks, Facebook offers more than one way to upload photos. In addition, you can use third-party applications that some Facebook members find faster and more convenient. In the following sections, you get to check out the various methods and choose the one you like best.

> **POKE**
>
> *Uploading* and *downloading* are fancy words for *copying*. The direction, up or down, is relative to you. If you're copying something from somewhere else to the device you're using, you're downloading. If you're copying from the device you're using to somewhere else, you're uploading.

Uploading Photos to a New Album

To upload your photos to a new photo album using Facebook's Photo Uploader, here's what you do:

1. Click **facebook** or **Home** in the blue bar at the top.

2. Click **Photos** (left menu).

3. Click **+ Upload Photos**. If the Select Photos to Upload option appears, go to step 4. If the Open dialog box appears, skip to step 5.

4. If prompted, click **Select Photos to Upload**. The Open dialog box appears prompting you to select photos.

5. Select the folder (on your computer) where the photos are stored. Facebook displays the photos in the selected folder.

Select the photos you want to upload.

6. Select the photos you want to upload just as you would select files on your computer.

7. Click the **Save** button. Facebook starts uploading the selected photos and displays the progress. Uploading might take several minutes depending on the number of photos, their size and quality, and the speed of your internet connection. When uploading is complete, you can enter a name for the new photo album and information about the photos in that album.

8. Highlight **Album Title** and type a descriptive name for the album.

9. (Optional) Click in the **Where were these taken** box and type the location where the photos were taken. You can click **Add Date** to stamp a date on them.

10. To include high-resolution photos, click the **High Quality** option.

11. (Optional) Below each photo, click **Say something about this photo** and type a description of it. You can also click the buttons below each photo to tag people in it, add a date, or specify the place it was taken.

12. Open the privacy list and click the option that describes whom you want to share the album with: **Public**, **Friends**, **Custom**, or friends on a specific friend list. If you choose Custom, use the resulting screen to enter your preferences.

13. Click or don't click **Post Photos**. Either way, Facebook creates the album and saves the photos to your account. If you post the photos and choose to share them with your friends, an update appears in your Timeline and News Feed to keep your friends posted. If you click your browser's Back button to avoid posting, then the album is saved for only your eyes to see—you can always choose to share it later.

Name the album   Specify a place and date

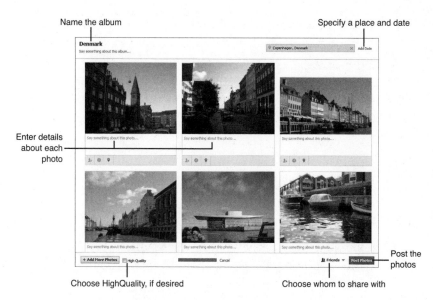

Enter details about each photo

Choose HighQuality, if desired   Choose whom to share with

Post the photos

Create an album in which to store this set of photos.

Uploading Photos to an Existing Album

If you already have a photo album and want to add more photos to it, click your name or profile picture in the blue bar and then click the **Photos** thumbnail. Click the album into which you want to upload more photos, and then click the **Add Photos** button (upper right). This starts Facebook's Photos Uploader, which you can use to upload additional photos as explained in the previous section starting with step 4. The process is a little less involved because you're not creating a new album.

To find out how to upload photos from your cell phone or other mobile device, head to Chapter 14.

Editing Your Photos and Albums

After uploading photos to an album on Facebook, you can edit the album or the photos it contains to add information about each photo, rearrange the photos in the album, delete photos, and more.

To get started, click your name or profile picture in the blue bar, click your **Photos** thumbnail, click **See All**, and click the album you want to work with. Facebook displays thumbnails of all the photos in that album. On this screen, you can drag and drop thumbnails to rearrange photos in the album or click a photo to display it on its own page, as explained in the next section.

Drag and drop to
rearrange photos   Edit the album   Add photos

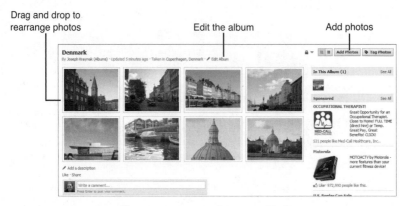

You can rearrange photos or add photos.

Click the **Edit Album** link just above the thumbnails. The album editing window appears, enabling you to change the album name, add a location and description, and change the privacy setting for the album. This window also provides a trashcan button you can click to delete the album. Buttons that appear below each image enable you to tag people in the photo, specify the date the photo was taken, and add a location.

You can customize the album, edit its photos, or delete it.

Working on Individual Photos

You can do a great deal of customizing in the Edit Album page, but some options are unavailable unless you view an image on its own page. To view an image solo, click your name or profile picture in the blue bar, click the **Photos** thumbnail, click the album that contains the image, and then click the image.

In this view, you can take the following actions:

- **Tag Photo:** Click **Tag Photo**, click someone in the photo, and enter the person's name. See the next section for more about tagging photos.

- **Add a description:** Click **Add a Description** or click the **Edit** button, and type a description of the photo. You can also specify who you were with and where you took the photo.

- **Add Location:** Click **Add Location**, start typing the name of the location, and if Facebook displays the right match, click it. If Facebook doesn't display the right match, arrow down to **Add Place "<Name>"**, press **Enter**, and use the Add Place dialog box to add the location.

- **Edit:** Click **Edit** to add a description, specify who you were with and the date on which the photo was taken, and a location. When you're done, click **Done Editing**.

- **Like:** Click **Like** to indicate that you like the photo and let your friends know you like it. Who can see what you Like depends on the privacy settings you've entered.

- **Comment:** Click in the **Write a comment** box, type your comment, and press **Enter**.

- **Follow/Unfollow Post:** Click **Follow Post** or **Unfollow Post** to toggle the option on or off. If you follow a post, you receive a notification whenever someone comments on the photo, likes it, or tags someone in it.

- **Share:** Click **Share** to post the photo on your Timeline, a friend's Timeline, in a group, or on a Facebook page or send it as a private message. When you click **Share**, the Share this Photo dialog box appears, enabling you to type a message and select your share preferences.

- **Rotate Photo:** Mouse over the image to display additional
  options below it, click **Options**, and click **Rotate Left** or
  Rotate Right.

- **Make Profile Picture.** Mouse over the image to display
  additional options below it, click **Options**, and click **Make
  Profile Picture** to use this photo as the profile picture for
  your account.

- **Delete Photo:** To remove the photo from the album,
  mouse over the image to display additional options below
  it, click **Options**, click **Delete This Photo**, and click
  Confirm when prompted.

Do more with individual photos.

Tagging Photos

Facebook lets you tag photos (yours or your friends') to identify
people in those photos. Anyone viewing the photo can then mouse
over people shown in the photo to view the tag. Whenever you tag a
photo, the action is recorded in your News Feed, so your friends will
know when you've tagged yourself or one of them. If you tag one of
your Facebook friends, Facebook sends the person a notification and
posts it in the person's News Feed.

You can tag an album or an individual photo. To tag an album, click the album to display its contents, click the **Tag Photos** button in the upper-right corner, start typing the name of a friend or Facebook page you want to tag in the photo, and click the friend's or page's name when Facebook displays the correct match. When you're done entering tags, click **Save Tags**.

To tag a photo, here's what you do:

1. Click the album and then the photo you want to tag inside the album.

2. Click **Tag Photo**.

3. Position the mouse pointer (crosshairs) over the center of the person's face for the most accurate placement of your tag and click. The Tag box appears, in which you can do one of the following.

   - Choose your Facebook friend's name from the list provided.

   - Click in the **Type any name** box and start typing the name of the person or object. As you type, the list of friend names narrows to match what you've typed so far, and you can click a name in the list. If you're tagging a person (or object) who isn't a Facebook friend, just finish typing the name. (You can add the person's email address to invite him to join Facebook and see the photo you just tagged him in.)

4. Repeat steps 2 and 3 to tag other people and objects in the photo.

5. Click **Done Tagging**.

Start typing
the person's
name

Click the
right match

Tag yourself or your friends in photos.

WHOA!

Some people don't appreciate being tagged in photos, particularly if they think the photo captured them in an unflattering light, embarrassing pose, or hanging out with the wrong people, so be careful. If a friend removes a tag or requests that you remove a photo, respect her wishes. If a friend keeps tagging you in photos and you want that to stop, send your friend a message asking her to cease and desist (diplomatically, of course). If she continues, consider unfriending her so she won't be able to tag you. For more about unfriending, check out Chapter 4. One more thing: don't even think about using tags to advertise or promote a product or service.

You can remove a tag at any time. Display the tagged photo, click **Edit**, and click the **X** next to the name of the person tagged in the photo.

Managing Your Photos with Third-Party Applications

Facebook is actually ill-equipped to handle photos. Sure, you can upload photos and share them with your friends, but Facebook lacks the file-management and photo-editing tools present in dedicated photo-management services like Flickr and Picasa. As a result, you tend to see a lot of bad photos on Facebook—photos that are too dark, too light, have red-eye issues, and so on.

Because Facebook lacks the essential photo-enhancement tools, consider using a full-featured program or service and linking it to your Facebook account. Facebook includes applications for the most popular photo-sharing services, including Flickr and Picasa, which enable you to upload photos directly to Facebook. The following sections show you how.

Linking to Picasa

Google features an excellent photo-management program called *Picasa* that you can download (it's free!) and use on your computer to manage your photos, edit them to look just right, and upload them into Picasa web folders (on Google). With the addition of the Picasa Uploader application for Facebook, you can edit the photos on your computer in Picasa and then upload them directly to your albums on Facebook—and even create new albums.

To learn more about Picasa and download and install your free copy of the program, visit picasa.google.com.

After installing Picasa, take the following steps to install the Picasa Uploader for Facebook:

1. Close your web browser and restart it. Otherwise, if you try to install the Picasa plugin, Facebook won't recognize your recent Picasa installation and won't allow you to continue.

2. Go to apps.facebook.com/picasauploader.

3. Click **Install Now** and follow the on-screen instructions to complete the installation. This adds a button to Picasa that enables you to upload photos directly from Picasa to Facebook.

When you're ready to upload photos from Picasa to Facebook, select the photos in Picasa as you normally do and then click the **Facebook** button. The Facebook Uploader dialog box appears. Click **Start Upload**.

Select the photos you want to upload

Click the Facebook button

You can upload photos directly from Picasa to Facebook.

Linking to Flickr

Yahoo!'s Flickr is the most popular service dedicated exclusively to digital photo sharing. Go to www.flickr.com, register for the service (it's free), and you can instantly begin uploading your photos. (To find additional tools for enhancing your Flickr experience, including the Flickr Uploadr for your desktop, visit www.flickr.com/tools.)

After uploading photos to Flickr, you can easily share them on Facebook. Display the photo you want to share and click the **Facebook** button just above the image. When the Request for Permission dialog box appears, click **Allow** to give your permission. Flickr displays another dialog box that enables you to add a message. Type a message, if desired, and click **Post**. The image is posted to your Timeline and News Feed.

Click the Facebook button

ScannedImage-8

Share your Flickr photos on Facebook.

If you want to share your Flickr photos on Facebook as you upload them to Flickr, you can link your Flickr and Facebook accounts. Here's how:

1. Create a Flickr account if you don't yet have one and sign in to your account.

2. Click your username near the upper-right corner of Flickr to display your account information.

3. Click the **Sharing & Extending** tab.

4. Click the **Connect** button in the Facebook box. A window appears prompting you to confirm.

5. Click **Allow**.

Now, whenever you upload photos to Flickr and choose to make them public, the photos are automatically posted to your Facebook account. To unlink the two accounts, display your Flickr account settings again, click the **Sharing & Extending** tab, click the **Edit** button next to Facebook, and choose to remove the connection.

The Least You Need to Know

- To access your photos, click your name or profile picture in the top menu and then click your **Photos** thumbnail.
- To create a photo album, go to your Timeline, click the **Photos** thumbnail, click **+ Upload Photos**, and follow the on-screen prompts.
- To view photos in one of your albums, go to your Timeline, click the **Photos** thumbnail, and click the album.
- Click a photo in your album to display it on a page of its own. From there, you can change the description, add a comment, rotate the photo, tag people or objects shown in the photo, delete the photo, or make it your Profile photo.
- To tag yourself or a friend in a photo, click the photo to display it on its own page, click **Tag Photo**, click the person, start typing a name, and then click the right match or press **Enter**.

Uploading and Sharing Video Footage

In This Chapter

- Viewing your friends' video clips
- Adhering to Facebook's video guidelines
- Sharing your own video clips with friends
- Editing your video clips
- Getting personal with video email

YouTube might be the leader in video hosting and sharing, but Facebook is no slouch in this arena. Members can upload video clips, post video clips on their Timelines, tag and comment on clips, post notes with video, and even record footage directly to Facebook using a webcam!

Whether you're an indie filmmaker looking to spread the word about your new feature film or a proud parent wanting to share Junior's first steps with your extended family, this chapter helps you project your footage onto your Timeline and share it on Facebook.

Viewing Other People's Video Clips

You don't have to fire up your camcorder to start enjoying Facebook's video features. If you have any filmmakers among your Facebook friends, you can watch their videos. In the following sections, we show you how to watch a video clip and comment on it, tag yourself or your Facebook friends in clips, and watch any videos in which you've been tagged.

POKE

To watch videos on Facebook, you'll need the latest Flash Player (available at www.adobe.com/products/flashplayer).

Watching a Video Clip

Whenever one of your friends posts a video, it appears in your News Feed, including a thumbnail of the video along with a play button. Click the **Play** button or anywhere on the thumbnail to run the video. Facebook enlarges the viewer and starts playing the clip.

Play button ——

*Click **Play**.*

To check out whether one of your Facebook friends has recorded and uploaded any video, check out your friend's Video page by following these steps:

1. Head to your friend's Timeline. (You can use the Search box or the Friends box on your Timeline to track down a friend.)

2. Click the **Photos** below the friend's cover image.

3. Just above your friend's photos, click the **Videos** link.

4. Click the video you want to watch. Facebook starts playing the video on its own page.

Click the video you want to play

Watch a friend's video.

Commenting on a Video

Wherever you happen to find a friend's video, you're likely to find a **Write a comment...** box. Click inside the box, type your comment, and press **Enter**.

You can always delete one of your own comments by clicking **X** (Remove) next to your comment.

WHOA!

If you don't see a Write a comment... box, it means someone other than one of your Facebook friends posted the clip or the Facebook member who posted the clip has a privacy setting that prohibits you from commenting on the clip.

Tagging a Video

If a video includes cameo appearances of you or your friends, consider tagging the video to let people know who's in it. When you tag a video, the name of the person you tagged appears below it, and Facebook notifies your friend that he's been tagged. If you tag yourself, that recent activity might appear in your News Feed to keep your friends posted.

To tag one of your own videos, first display it on its own page (by clicking on it). Click **Tag This Video**, click in the **Who were you with?** box, and then start typing the name of a Facebook friend who appears in the video. As you type, the list of friend names narrows to match what you've typed so far, and you can click a name in the list. To enter another name, press **Enter** or **Return** and then enter the next name. When you're done, click **Done Editing**. (To remove the tag, repeat the steps and delete the person's name.)

The process for tagging someone else's video is nearly the same. Click the video to display it on its own page, click **Tag This Video**, start typing the name of a Facebook friend who appears in the video, click the person's name, and click Save.

Enter the names of friends to tag

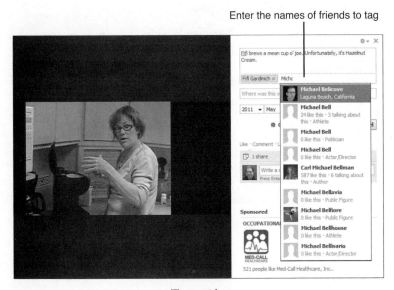

Tag a video.

Watching Videos in Which You've Been Tagged

Turnabout is fair play. Just as you can tag your Facebook friends in videos, they can tag you. If you happen to get tagged, Facebook sends you a notification so you can check out the video. To view all the videos in which you've been tagged, take the following steps:

1. Click your name or profile picture (in the top menu bar). Facebook displays your Timeline.

2. Click **Photos** below your cover image. Your Photos page appears. If you've been tagged in any videos, your Photos page should contain a Videos of You box.

3. In the Videos of You box, click the video you want to watch. The video appears on its own page.

4. Click the video to play it.

You can't remove the tag yourself, but you can mouse over your name in the video's description to see who tagged you and then click the person's name to access his or her Timeline and send the person a message. If the person fails to comply with your request to remove the tag, you can unfriend or report and/or block the person.

You can view all videos in which you've been tagged.

Recording and Uploading Video Footage

With a digital camcorder or a webcam, you have all the equipment you need to shoot your own video footage. With Facebook's assistance, you can then upload your video to the web and share it with your friends.

In the following sections, we briefly explain Facebook's video guide-lines and then show you how to access your Video page, upload video clips stored on your computer, record videos with a webcam, and edit some of the details related to your clip.

Taking Note of Facebook's Video Guidelines

Facebook isn't YouTube. You can't just upload any video footage you think is cool. To keep the spotlight focused on friends, Facebook stipulates that any video clips you choose to upload meet the following conditions:

- Compliant with the Facebook Code of Conduct and Terms of Use. The term of use Facebook probably had in mind here is this one: "You will not post content that is hateful, threatening, or pornographic; incites violence; or contains nudity or graphic or gratuitous violence."

- Personal in nature. Videos must be of you or your friends, taken by you or your friends, or original art or animation created by you or your friends.

- Does not infringe upon or violate the copyright, trademark, publicity, privacy, or other rights of any third party.

- Does not attempt to circumvent any filtering techniques or technologies Facebook might use to screen content.

WHOA!

If you post video that doesn't adhere to every single one of these guidelines, Facebook may remove the content and perhaps even terminate your account.

Accessing the Video Page

Facebook features everything you need to upload and share video, and all the tools are accessible via the Create a New Video page. To get to there from your Home page, click **Photos** (in the left menu), and then click the **+ Upload video** button above the photos. The Create a New Video page appears.

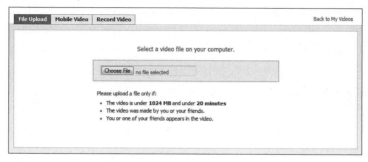

You can record and upload video via the Create a New Video page.

Uploading a Video Clip from Your Computer

If you have any digital video clips lying around on your computer, you can upload them to Facebook. The only limitation (besides Facebook's Code of Conduct) is that the video can be no longer than 20 minutes and no larger than 1024MB (1 gigabyte).

Facebook supports numerous digital video formats, including Mobile Video (*.3g2, *.3gp, *.3gpp), DIVX Video (*.divx), DV Video (*.dv), Windows Media Video (*.asf and *.wmv), AVI Video (*.avi), Flash Video (*.flv, *.f4v), MPEG Video (*.mpeg, *.mpe, *.mpg, *.dat), MPEG-4 Video (*.m4v, *.mp4, *.mpeg4), Matroska Format (*.mkv), MOD Video (*.mod), QuickTime Movie (*.mov, *.qt), Nullsoft Video (*.nsv), Ogg Format (*.ogm, *.ogv), TOD (*.tod), M2TS Video (*.m2ts), AVCHD (*.mts), MPEG Transport Stream (*.ts), and DVD Video (*.vob).

To upload a digital video file from your computer, take the following steps:

1. Head to your Home page and click the **Photo** tab.

2. Click **+ Add Videos** (upper-right corner). The Create a New Video page appears.

3. Click **Browse** or **Choose File**. A dialog box appears prompting you to choose the video file(s) you want to upload.

4. Navigate to the folder where the digital video file is stored, select the file, and click **Open**. Facebook starts uploading it and displays a form you can fill out while you're waiting. (If this is the first time you're uploading video, Facebook may prompt you to agree to the terms of service.)

5. Enter any information you want to include with the video, including a title, description, a list of people in the video, and privacy settings to determine who can and can't view the video.

6. Click **Save Info**.

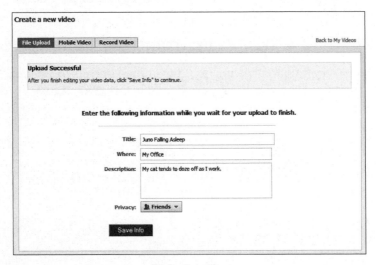

Upload a video.

For instructions on how to upload videos from your cell phone or other mobile device, see Chapter 15.

Recording Video Using Your Webcam

If you're in the mood to make and post live video, plug a webcam into your computer, and you instantly convert it into a digital video recorder. With the addition of Facebook, you can now film yourself on the fly and instantly upload the clip to Facebook. Here's what you do:

1. Head to your Home page and click the **Photos** tab.

2. Click **+ Add Videos** (upper-right corner). The Create a New Video page appears.

3. Click the **Record Video** tab. The Adobe Flash Player Settings dialog box appears, asking permission to access your camera and microphone.

4. Click **Allow** and then **Close**. A window appears, showing what your webcam sees right now.

5. Click the **Record** button (the red button with the white dot, last we checked), and then proceed to ham it up in front of the camera. (After you click the Record button, it changes into a Stop button.)

6. When you're done with the show, click the **Stop** button.

7. Click **Play** to view the video.

8. Take one of the following steps:
   • If you don't like the clip, click **Reset** and head back to step 5 for a reshoot.
   • If you like the clip, click **Save**. This takes you to the Edit Video page, where you can enter information about the video.

9. Enter any information you want to include with the video, including a title, description, and privacy settings to determine who can and can't view the video. You can also choose a frame of the video to serve as the thumbnail that represents it.

10. Click **Save**. Facebook saves your video and posts it to your Timeline and News Feed to share with friends.

FRIEND-LY ADVICE

When recording, try to look at the camera rather than the screen. Otherwise, you appear to be looking away from your audience.

Film yourself live!

Editing Video Information

After you upload or record a video, you can edit any information you entered and make other changes, such as rotating the clip 90 degrees clockwise or counterclockwise (if you shot it at an angle).

To edit the video, click **Home** (in the top menu), click the **Photos** tab on the left, click **My Albums**, click the **Videos** link (above your photos), and then click the video you want to edit. This displays the video on its own page, where you can select any of the following options:

- **Tag this video:** Click **Tag this video** and start typing the person's name. If Facebook displays the name of the friend you want to tag, click it. If Facebook doesn't find a match, finish typing the name and press **Enter**.

- **Embed this video:** Click **Embed this video** to obtain an HTML tag you can use to insert the video on a web page or in a blog entry.

- **Like:** Click **Like** to indicate that you like the video and let your friends know you like it. Who can see what you Like depends on the privacy settings you've entered.

- **Comment:** Click in the **Write a comment** box, type your comment, and press **Enter**.

- **Follow/Unfollow Post:** Click **Follow Post** or **Unfollow Post** to toggle the option on or off. If you follow a post, you receive a notification whenever someone comments on the video, likes it, or tags someone in it.

- **Share:** Click **Share** to post the video on your Timeline, a friend's Timeline, in a group, or on a Facebook page or send it as a private message. When you click **Share**, the Share this video dialog box appears, enabling you to type a message and select your share preferences.

- **Edit:** Click **Edit** to enter additional details about the video, including a description of it, names of people who are in the video, where the video was shot, and who can view the video.

- **Rotate video:** Mouse over the video, click **Options**, which appears below the video when you mouse over it, and click **Rotate Left** or **Rotate Right**.

- **Change the date:** Mouse over the video, click **Options**, click **Change Date**, and enter a date for the video.

- **Delete Video:** To remove the video, mouse over the video, click **Options**, click **Delete Video**, and click **Delete** when prompted to confirm.

Edit information about the video.

Embedding a Video

If you have your own website or blog, you can embed your Facebook videos on your web pages or include them in your blog posts. Here's what you do:

1. Click **Home** (in the top menu), click the **Photos** tab on the left, click **My Albums**, click the **Videos** link (above your photos), and then click the video you want to embed. The video appears on a page of its own.

2. Click **Embed this Video**. The Embed Your Video box appears.

3. Click in the **Embed code** text box to highlight the code and then press **Ctrl+C** (on a PC) or **Command+C** (on a Mac), to copy it.

4. Open the web page or blog post in which you want to embed the video in HTML view. Web authoring and blogging software typically enable you to edit content in HTML mode (where you can see the tags) or in Visual mode (where the page looks like it will appear to users). In WordPress, for example, you click the **HTML** tab to edit in HTML mode. If you paste the <embed> code in Visual mode, people see the code instead of the video.

5. Click where you want to embed the video.

6. Press **Ctrl+V** (on a PC) or **Command+V** (on a Mac) to insert the embed code.

7. Save your web page or blog post.

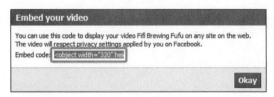

You can embed a Facebook video on a web page or blog post.

Whenever someone views your web page or blog post, a small box appears with a Play button inside it that the visitor can click to play the video. The cool thing is that, because the video is stored on Facebook and not on your web-hosting service, none of your resources are required to play the video—in other words, you're not using up any of your storage space or bandwidth.

Sending a Video Message via Email

Tired of sending plain text messages? Add some spark with a video clip. On Facebook, it's easy—especially if you already uploaded or recorded a clip. To send a video that's already on Facebook (your own video or a Facebook friend's), here's what you do:

1. Display the video on its own page. For example, click **Home**, **Photos**, **My Albums**, **Videos**, and then click the video you want to share via email; or you can click a video in your News Feed and then click its title (below the video).

2. Click the **Share** link. The Share this video box opens.

3. Open the Share menu (upper left) and click **In a private message**.

4. Click in the **Enter a friend's name** box and enter the name(s) of one or more Facebook friends.

5. Click in the **Write something** box and type a message to accompany the video. It's always a good idea to let people know why they might like to watch it.

6. Click **Share video**.

You can send a video clip as a message attachment to your Facebook friends.

The Least You Need to Know

- To access videos, head to a Timeline (your own or a friend's), click the **Photos** thumbnail, and click the **Videos** link.

- To tag a video, display it on its own page, click **Tag This Video**, enter the names of the friends you want to tag, and click **Done Editing**.

- Videos on Facebook can't contain content that is hateful, threatening, or pornographic, or that contains nudity or graphic or gratuitous violence. In addition, any video you post must be shot by you or a Facebook friend and contain you or at least one of your Facebook friends.

- In the upper-right corner of your Video page is a button for adding video.

- To comment on a video, click in the **Write a comment...** box, type your comment, and press **Enter**.

- The Share option next to a video enables you to post the video to your News Feed or send it as a message attachment to your friends.

Gathering and Sharing in Groups

In This Chapter

- Exploring group dynamics on Facebook
- Joining and leaving groups
- Sharing photos, videos, and other cool stuff
- Creating your own group and gathering members
- Engaging in group chats and collaborative writing

You and your friends on Facebook form a tightly knit clique, but Facebook also enables you to wander off and mingle more intimately with friends and others in *groups*. Groups are useful for gathering former classmates; sharing information among family members; meeting people who share similar goals, values, or interests; facilitating communication among members of an organization; and so on. And you don't even have to be Facebook friends to do it.

In this chapter, we show you how to join a group, form your own groups, engage in discussions, and share stuff with your fellow group members.

Understanding Groups: Open, Closed, and Secret

Facebook Groups are like gatherings around the water cooler, where you can wander away from your News Feed and Timeline to enter discussions and share with friends and non-friends alike in a more theme-oriented environment. On Facebook, you can create or join the following three types of groups:

- **Open:** Open groups enable Facebook members—friends and non-friends—to share common interests and passions. They're great for promoting a political candidate, organizing a movement, or even networking with people in a particular field.

- **Closed:** Exclusive areas where only selected Facebook friends hang out. For example, you can create a closed group for the South Vernon High School class of 1998 and allow only members of that class to join.

- **Secret:** Super-secret, invitation-only clubs that don't even show up in Facebook search results. Secret groups are great for when you don't want outsiders on Facebook knowing what you're up to.

FRIEND-LY ADVICE

If you're working on a project with others, you can create a secret work group where members can discuss ideas, collaborate on solving problems, monitor progress, and schedule meetings.

Exploring Existing Groups

The first encounter most Facebook members have with Groups is when they receive an invitation from a friend to join a group. (We provide more information about responding to such invitations later in this chapter.) However, you don't need to wait for an invitation to get involved in group activities. You can be more proactive by browsing groups or searching for groups that interest you.

Searching for a Group

If you'd like to check out groups that focus on a specific interest or topic, search for groups by keyword or phrase. Here's how:

1. Click in the **Search** box (in the top menu), type a keyword or two or three, and then click the **Search** button (the one with the magnifying glass on it) or press **Enter.** Facebook displays the top items that match your search entry. The search results may include people, groups, pages, posts by friends, and other items.

2. Click **Groups** (in the left menu).

3. Scroll down the list to browse available groups that match your search criteria.

4. When you reach the bottom of the list, you can click **See More Results** to view the next 10 groups in the list.

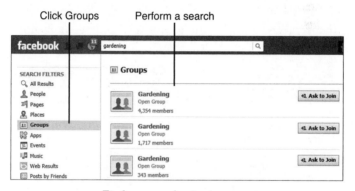

Find a group that interests you.

Finding Groups Through Your Friends

Chances are good that if one of your close Facebook friends joins a group, it's worth checking out. Friends can turn you on to groups in the following ways:

- **Invitation:** A friend can send you an invitation to join the group. Accept the invitation, and you're in.

- **Your News Feed:** Whenever a friend joins a group, that activity might show up in your News Feed with a link to the group, unless your friend chose to remove that item from his Recent Activity area after joining the group. Click the link to head to the group's Home page.

- **Friends' Timelines:** Whenever someone joins a group, the activity is posted on the person's Timeline under Recent Activities. By pulling up a friend's Timeline and scrolling down to Recent Activities, you can check out which groups your friend has recently joined.

To find out how to prevent the Groups app from posting updates to your News Feed or to hide the fact that you joined a particular group, skip ahead to the section "Joining a Group."

Checking Out a Group

After you've found a few groups that possibly match your interests, you can inspect them more closely. Click the group's name or the picture that represents it, and the group's Home page pops up.

An open group's Home page lets you sample the group before joining it.

A closed group's Home page severely restricts access for nonmembers. You might see some basic information, but you probably won't see discussions or the group's member list until you join.

Getting Involved in a Group

To get involved in a group and share with its members, you must first join the group. As you see in the following sections, joining and leaving a group are two of the easiest things you can do on Facebook.

Joining a Group

All you need to do to join an open group on Facebook is click the **Join Group** button for the group you want to join; its located near the upper-right corner of the group's page. You then have to wait for one of the group's administrators to confirm your request. You don't have to keep checking; when you're allowed in, you receive a notification letting you know. If your request is denied or ignored, you don't receive notification.

If you click the Join Group button and then decide not to join before you're accepted into the group, access the group's Home page and click **Cancel Request** (near the upper-right corner).

Leaving a Group

If you happen to lose interest in a group, you can leave at any time. Click the **Groups** icon (in the left menu). Click the name of the group you want to leave, click the gear icon near the upper-right corner of the group's page, and click **Leave Group**. When prompted to confirm, click **Leave Group**. That's it. You're outta there. If you're the only member of the group and you leave, the group disappears.

Conversing in Groups

Posting content to a group is no different than posting content to your Timeline or News Feed. When you're ready to post a message to the group, click in the **Write something...** box, type your message, and click **Post**.

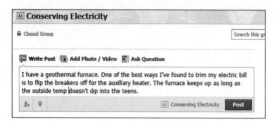

Share with the group.

In addition to posting status updates, you can post a link, photo, video clip, or question just as you can on your Timeline or News Feed. Just click one of the following icons in the Publisher:

- **Add photo/video:** To share a photo or video with the group, click **Add photo/video** and then click **Upload photo/video, Use webcam,** or **Create photo album** to add a photo or video to share. See Chapters 7 and 8 for more about sharing photos and video on Facebook.

- **Ask question:** Click **Ask question**, click in the **Ask something** box, and type your question. To poll the group, click **Add Poll Options** and use the **Add an option** selections to provide answer choices. Click **Post** to post your question.

You can also add a link to a post simply by typing or pasting the website address of the page you want to link to. After you type the address, Facebook displays the page title and description and gives you the opportunity to choose a thumbnail for the link or choose **No thumbnail**. At this point, you can delete the page address and type something about the link to introduce it.

POKE

You can attach a link, photo, or video clip to your status update before or after composing your text entry, or you can omit the text entry and post the item without adding any commentary.

As a member of a group, you receive a notification whenever someone comments on something you posted. If these notifications get annoying, you can unfollow the post. Just go to the group, find the conversation, and click its **Unfollow post** link. The Unfollow post link turns into the Follow post link, which you can click if you change your mind.

Creating Your Own Group

If you can find a Facebook group that serves your interests and needs, then join it. Numerous similar groups merely dilute interests and enthusiasm. If you can't find a group that addresses your interests and meets your needs, you can create your own group. Here's how:

1. From your Home page, click **Create group...** (in the left menu). The Create Group dialog box appears.

2. Type a name for the group in the **Group name** box.

3. Click in the **Members** box, start typing the name of a friend to add to the group, and when you see the name you want, click it. Continue to type and click to add more names.

4. Choose the type of group you want to create: Open, Closed, or Secret.

5. Click **Create**. Facebook creates the group. Group members' profile pictures appear at the top of the group's Home page.

Create a group.

From the group's Home page, you can change the group's settings by clicking the button with the gear on it (upper-right corner) and clicking **Edit Group**. You can change the group name, its privacy setting, and whether only administrators can approve requests to join; set up group email; or add a description of the group, which is always a good idea. When you're done making adjustments, click the Save button near the bottom.

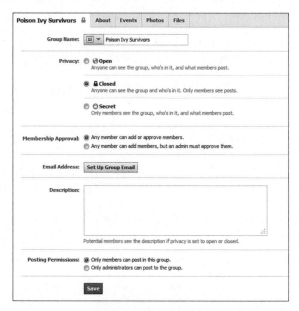

Edit your group settings.

Creating a Group Email Address

A group email address enables anyone in the group to send an email message to the address so Facebook distributes it to all group members. The email address will be <something>@groups.facebook. com, and you'll supply the "<something>." You can't change it, so think of a name that's short, descriptive, and easy to remember.

To create a group email address, go to your Home page and click the name of the group (in the left menu). Click the button with the gear on it, click **Edit Group**, and then click the **Set Up Group Email** button. Type the beginning of the email address (no spaces), such as group-name@groups.facebook.com, and then click **Create email address**.

Create a group email address.

Adding Friends to the Group

Although you added friends to the group when you first created it, you can add more friends at any time. Head to the group's page by clicking its name in the left menu on your Home page. Then, click **+ Add friends to group** in the column on the right. Start typing the name of a friend, and when you see the name you want, click it or arrow down to it and press **Tab**.

Add or remove group members.

Removing Group Members

If you're one of the group's administrators, you can kick someone out of the group. From your Home page, on the left menu, click the name of the group in which the person is a member. Click the **# Members** link near the top of the right column. Click the **X** next to the name/photo of the member you want to eject. The Remove box appears prompting you to confirm the removal. To ban the member permanently from the group, click **Ban Permanently**. When you're ready to do the deed, click **Confirm**.

To kick an administrator out of the group, you need to remove the person's administrator status first, as explained in the next section.

Making Someone Else an Administrator

When you create a group, you become its administrator. Only you have the power to edit the group and add people to and remove them from the group. If you'd like to share your administrator duties, you can make other group members administrators. Here's how:

1. On your Home page, click the name of the group (left menu).

2. Click **# Members** link, near the top of the right column. Facebook displays all of the group's members.

3. Click **Make Admin** next to the name/photo of the person to whom you want to grant administrator privileges.

You can always remove a member's administrator status. Just access the members list again and click **Remove Admin** next to the member's name.

> **POKE**
>
> Just above the Members list is a button you can click to sort the members list. Click the button and click **Admins** to view only the group members who are also administrators.

Sharing Photos Within the Group

You can share photos within a group that only those who belong to the group have access to. This is great if you create a group for your family or your graduating class and want to share photos privately.

To view or add photos, head to your Home page and click the group's name (in the left menu). In the right column, click the **Photos** tab, which is above the center column. From this page, you can check out any photo albums that group members have created or click **+ Upload Photos** to share photos with the group. For more about photo sharing, see Chapter 7.

Creating an Event

If you're planning a special event for the group, such as a monthly meeting, a reunion, or a holiday party, consider using the Facebook Event feature to invite everyone and keep track of who's planning to show up.

To announce an event, head to the group's page, click the **Events** tab (above the center column), and click **+ Create Event**. The Create an Event form appears. Enter the requested information, including a name for the event, the date and time, location, and details. By default, Facebook will invite all members of the group. If you want to be more selective, remove the checkmark next to **Invite members of the host group <name>**, and then click the **Select guests** button to invite your friends individually. You might also want to remove the checkmark next to **Make this event public**, so you don't end up with thousands of unwelcome guests, which could culminate in the ultimate of surprise parties. You also have the option to **Show the guest list on the Event page** and **Add event photo**. When you're done entering your preferences, click **Create event**.

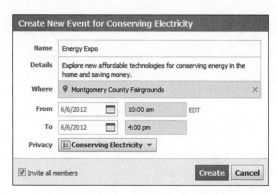

Create an event.

To edit the event, head to your Home page, click **Events** (in the left menu), click the event you want to edit, and click the **Edit** button.

For more about Facebook's Event feature, check out Chapter 10.

Chatting with the Group

Few things in life are more invigorating than chatting with a group, and now Facebook has made that possible. With Group Chat, everyone in the group can join the discussion as if you're all sitting in the same room. Nobody outside the group can "listen in" or intrude.

To start chatting, head to the group's page and click the chat window title bar in the lower-right corner. (If you don't see a chat window title bar for the group, click the button with the gear on it in the upper-right corner and click **Chat with group**.) A small chat window pops up from the bottom of the screen. Type something to get the conversation rolling and press **Enter**. Assuming other group members are online, logged in to Facebook, and available to chat, a chat window appears on their screens, too, and they can join in the conversation.

For more about Facebook Chat, see Chapter 6.

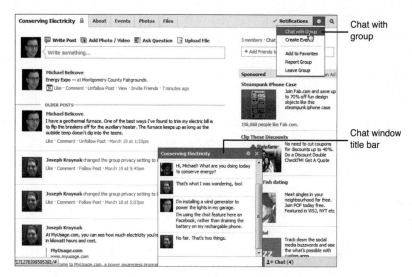

Chat with the group.

Collaborating on a Group Document

If your group is primarily work-related, you might need to collaborate on documents, and you can do so in a Facebook Group. To create a new document to start working on, access the group's page, click the **Files** tab (above the center column), click the button with the plus sign and down arrow on it, and click **Create a doc**.

Click in the **Title** box and type a name for the document. Click in the large blank area and start typing your draft. You can also paste contents into this area. When you're done composing your draft, click the **Create Doc** button. A post appears on the group's page along with a link for viewing the document. Any group member can click the link to preview the document and then click the **Edit Doc** link to view and edit it.

Click the **Files** tab at any time to view a list of group documents. Click the document's name to view it and then click **Edit Doc** (above the document's contents) to edit it.

The Least You Need to Know

- Groups enable you to mingle with Facebook friends and others and engage in discussions outside the more public venues of Timelines and News Feeds.

- To find groups that might interest you, click in the **Search** box (top menu), type a descriptive word or two for the type of group you want, press **Enter**, and then click **Groups** (left menu).

- To create a group, click **Home** (top menu), **Create Group...** (left menu), and follow the on-screen prompts.

- To join a group, click the **Ask to Join** button next to the group's name.

- On your Home page, the left menu contains links to all of the groups you belong to.

- Every group page has profile pictures of the members at the top along with four tabs: Members, Events, Photos, and Docs.

Finding and Scheduling Events

In This Chapter

* Meeting your own personal events planner
* Finding out what's happening
* Responding to an invitation
* Planning your own event and announcing it

> *Party at Mikal's house, Saturday night, 6 P.M. till ?:?? A.M., BYOB! Food, ice, and entertainment provided! Be sure to RSVP, so we know how much pizza to order!*

Yep, announcing an event on Facebook is as easy and inexpensive as that. No mailing invitations. No phone calls, wrong numbers, or answering machines. All you do is compose your event announcement, set your preferences, choose the friends you want to invite, and wait for them to RSVP or just show up. Whether you're planning a small get-together or a major public gathering like a benefit, concert, or grand opening, Facebook's Events app (application) has everything you need to spread the word, take a head count of likely attendees, and keep everyone in the loop regarding any change of plans.

If you're planning an upcoming event, this chapter can play a key role in your event planning. If you're just looking for something to do, you'll discover how to tune in to announcements of upcoming events and respond to any invitations you happen to receive.

Accessing and Navigating the Events App

Whenever you're planning an event or just in the mood for some action, head to the Events app. To get there from your Home page, click **Events** (in the left menu). The Events page appears, supplying you with a list of any events you've been invited to along with a link for creating an event. Consider the Events page your launchpad for doing everything else explained in this chapter.

Above the Events list are two important buttons: + Create Event and the button with the magnifying glass on it. Click the magnifying glass to filter the list to display upcoming, suggested, past, or declined events or birthdays or choose Export Events for instructions on how to export events to a calendar program, such as Microsoft Outlook or Apple iCal.

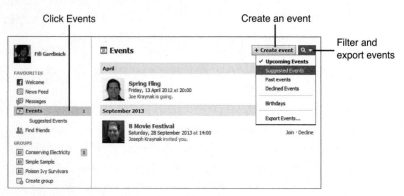

The Events app lets you check upcoming events and plan new events.

Click an event's title to find out more about it, including the date, time, and location; a full description of the event; a list of confirmed guests as well as people who've said they're not coming or might be coming and people who haven't yet responded to their invitations; any comments guests have chosen to post about the event; and options to join, maybe join, decline, share, and export the event. (We provide more details about responding to an invitation later in this chapter.)

See who's going
Accept invitation
Decline invitation
Indicate you may be coming

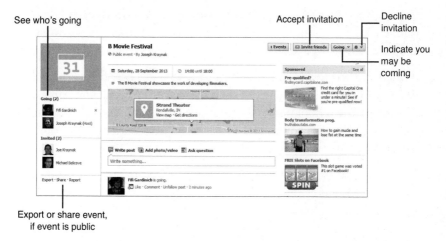

Export or share event, if event is public

Event details.

If you indicated that you're going or might be going and the event planner allows it, you can click the **Invite Friends** button (upper-right corner) to invite your friends. If the event planner chose not to allow guests to invite friends, the button doesn't appear.

Change whether you're going or not
View more options

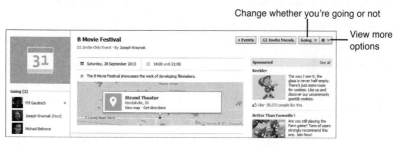

If you indicate you're going, you get more options.

Searching and Browsing Events

Bored? Nothing to do on a Friday night? Wrong! There's plenty going on. You just don't know about it. Now with Facebook, you can search for and browse events near or far to find potentially engaging activities.

Perhaps the best way to search for an event is to head to your Home page, click **Events**, and then use the Events page to check out what all your friends are doing.

To expand your horizons beyond what your Facebook friends are up to, you can search for events by type of event, the name of a band or comedian, a school name, location (city or town), special interest (like volleyball), and so on. Here's what you do to search for events:

1. Click in the **Search** box (top menu), type one or two words describing the sort of event you're interested in (for example, "slam poetry chicago").

2. At the bottom of the list that appears, click the **See more results for...** option. Facebook displays events, groups, pages, and other stuff that matches your search instructions.

3. Click **Events** (in the left menu). Facebook narrows the list to show only events related to the search entry.

Perform a broad search and then narrow the results to events only.

Responding to an Event Invitation

If you've been invited to an event or plan on attending an event open to the public, let the hosts know whether you're coming, not coming, or unsure. Besides being the polite thing to do, your response serves several practical purposes. For one, it helps the hosts take a head count, so they can prepare for the hungry, thirsty hordes who are likely to show up.

Perhaps more important, your response (especially if you're planning to attend) spreads the word about the event. Depending on your privacy settings, your response is likely to show up in your News Feed, Timeline, and in some cases—if you edit your Event preferences to allow for this—on all your friends' News Feeds. You also show up in the event's Confirmed Guests list and, as everyone knows, a crowd usually draws a crowd.

By letting the hosts know you're coming, you get a perk, too. If the hosts change plans or cancel the event and are responsible enough to make those changes on Facebook, you receive a notification on Facebook and via email (assuming you didn't disable email notifications for Events).

Letting the hosts know whether you're coming is a snap. Just head to the event's page and in the upper-right corner, click **Join**, **Maybe**, or **Decline**. If you received a personal invitation via email, you can use the same options to inform your hosts.

Click Join, Maybe, or Decline

Be polite by letting the event's host(s) know whether you're planning to attend.

FRIEND-LY ADVICE

Consider expressing your eager anticipation or whatever else on the event's page to get others excited about attending the event.

Announcing Your Own Special Event

Whether you're planning a family get-together, a slam poetry competition, or a political rally, you need to get the word out to your people. The easiest way to do this is to create an event on Facebook. All you do is specify the who, what, when, where, and why and then select the friends you want to invite. Facebook does the rest, sending out all your invitations in the blink of an eye. If plans change, just edit the event, and Facebook notifies everyone on your guest list!

In the following sections, we show you how to create and customize an event, invite guests, take a head count, print a guest list, and more. And in the unfortunate circumstance that your event fizzles, we even show you how to cancel it.

FRIEND-LY ADVICE

Be polite. Don't invite people you don't really know to a highly personal event like a birthday party or baby shower. If you're coordinating an event, don't overpromote it or send too many reminders to your friends.

Creating an Event

Creating an event is easy. Start the process using one of the following methods, depending on whether you're planning the event for your Facebook friends or for a Facebook Group you administer:

- **Event for Friends:** From your Home page, click **Events** (in the left menu). Click **+ Create Event**. The Create New Event dialog box appears, prompting you to enter details about the event.

- **Group Event:** Pull up the group's page, as explained in Chapter 9, click the **Event** tab (upper-right corner), and then click **+ Create Event**. By creating the event from the group's page, you'll have the option to invite all group members simply by clicking a check box.

However you choose to initiate the process, the Create an Event screen appears, prompting you to enter details about the event. Specify the event's date and time, add a brief description of the event, enter its location, and use the Details box to enter additional details. When specifying a location, this is typically a name of a place everyone you're inviting is familiar with. If you're not sure whether everyone is familiar with it, click in the **Where** box and type a street address and the name of the city or town.

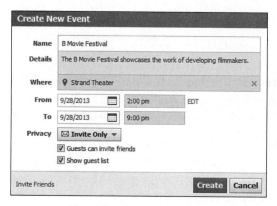

Enter details about the event.

WHOA!

Think twice about entering contact information in your event description. People can contact you through Facebook. You don't need to risk having your email address or phone number fall into the wrong hands.

When you're done entering details about the event, click **Invite Friends,** click the people you want to invite, enter email addresses of anyone you want to invite who's not a Facebook member, and click **Save**. If you're creating a group event, you'll see the following options:

- **Invite members of the host group <name>:** This option appears only if you're creating a Facebook Group event. It enables you to easily invite all group members.

- **Make this event public:** Unless you want to open this event to everyone on Facebook, uncheck this option. If you uncheck it, another option appears: guests can invite Friends. You probably want to make sure this option is deselected, too. If you want friends to be able to bring a significant other, you might add that to the Details box.

- **Show the guest list on the Event page:** To keep everyone posted as to who's been invited and plans on attending, make sure this option is checked.

To display similar options for a nongroup event, head to the event's page and click the **Edit** button (upper-right corner).

To add a photo for the event, click the **+ Add Event Photo** button, and use the resulting dialog box to upload a photo. We recommend adding a photo if for no other reason than to make the event seem more festive.

When you're done fleshing out your event, click the **Create Event** or **Save Event** button. Facebook displays the event's page and sends invitations to all of the invitees.

Carefully inspect your event for any errors. If you see something that's not right, click the **Edit** button, enter your changes, and click **Save Event**. (If you wandered off to do something else on Facebook, you can always pull up your event from your Home page by clicking **Events** in the left menu and then clicking the name of the event.)

Your event is born.

Keeping Your Guests in the Loop

As the date and time for the event nears, keep your guests excited about it and let them know of any changes in plans. You can do this by posting to the event's page or by messaging the guests directly. Post to the event's page to generate buzz. You might want to send a message instead to inform guests of any important changes, such as a change in date, time, or venue (location).

To send a message, head to the event's page, click the button with the gear on it (upper-right corner), and click **Message Guests**. By default, Facebook addresses the message to **All**, meaning everyone you invited. To change that, open the Attendees list and select your preference: **Attending**, **Maybe Attending**, or **Not Yet Replied**. Click in the **Message** box, type your message, and then click the **Send** button.

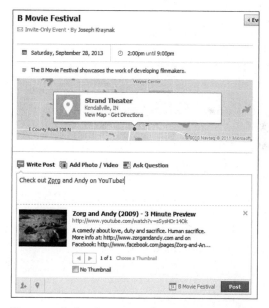

Post text, links, photos, or video to the event's Wall.

The Least You Need to Know

- To fire up the Events app from your Home page, click the **Events** icon in the left menu.

- On the Events page, click the button with the magnifying glass on it (upper-right corner) to display options to view suggested events, birthdays, and past events.

- If you're invited to an event, be sure to respond. It's the polite thing to do and keeps you in the loop.

- Use the **Search** box in the top menu to search for events, and then click **Events** in the left menu to show only events in the search results.

- To schedule an event and invite your friends, click **Events** (left menu), click the **+ Create Event** button (upper right), and then follow the on-screen prompts.

Monitoring Usage: For Parents and Teachers

In This Chapter

- Checking Facebook's minimum age requirement
- Guidance for parents of teenage Facebook users
- Tips for teachers and other responsible adults
- Understanding Facebook shorthand that might raise red flags

Facebook is an excellent venue for teenagers to keep in touch with family and friends, but as with any public venue, parents and teachers must provide some degree of supervision and protection. Although a vast majority of Facebook users adhere to the terms of service and are not on Facebook to take advantage of others or cause harm, a small minority of users seem to have nothing better to do. In addition, teenagers, like adults, might become embroiled in bitter disputes and fall prey to temptations that pull them in the wrong directions.

As a parent or teacher, you need to know about the potential threats and take steps to keep those you care for out of harm's way. In this chapter, we show you how.

Recognizing Facebook's Minimum Age Requirement

Some time ago we read an article in a local newspaper announcing the winners of an essay contest. The essay topic was "child abuse," and one of the winners was a fifth grade girl who wrote an essay about internet safety focusing on her experiences on Facebook. Apparently she hadn't read the terms of service (ToS), which specifically prohibits anyone under the age of 13 from using Facebook. Log in to Facebook, scroll to the bottom of the page, click **Terms**, click **Statement of Rights and Responsibilities,** and you can read it yourself under section #4—Registration and Account Safety:

> 4(5) You will not use Facebook if you are under 13.

Her parents and teachers probably hadn't read the ToS, either. In short, if your child or a student in your class is under the age of 13 years, she should not use Facebook.

POKE

Assuming a child or adolescent enters his correct age, Facebook prohibits those who are under 13 from setting up an account. In addition, Facebook sets stricter default privacy settings for younger users, so less information is shared with the public. But keep in mind that Facebook members can adjust these settings.

Providing Parental Supervision

As a parent, the biggest step you can take toward protecting your teenager on Facebook is to be involved in your child's life. Be aware of what she is doing at home, school, after school, and on weekends; get to know her friends and her friends' parents; and foster an atmosphere of open communication, so your teenager feels comfortable talking to you when difficult situations arise. Following are some additional tips:

- If you're not on Facebook yet, join and remain active, so you develop an understanding of how it works and the available privacy and sharing features.

- Set ground rules and consequences. Ground rules might include specific hours when computer and cell phone use is permitted and prohibited, like at the dinner table and after bedtime. Consequences might include loss of rights to use the computer, tablet, or cell phone. We don't recommend shooting your teenager's laptop, as one father in the news chose to do.

- Engage in conversations with your teenager about Facebook in general and Facebook safety specifically. A good way to get your teen talking is to ask questions about your own account, such as how to set up your profile, how to change your privacy settings, and how to share what you post selectively.

- Require or ask your child whether you can friend her, and then be selective in posting to your child's Timeline, tagging your child, and so forth. If you're too much of a presence on your child's Facebook account, your child is likely to unfriend you or keep you out of the loop when posting by creating a List that includes everyone but you. Keep a low profile, and you have a better chance of being able to monitor activity.

- Encourage your teenager to share with care, letting him know that what he posts online has a greater potential than person-to-person interactions of being misinterpreted and shared with others. Also remind your teenager that what he shares on Facebook is a reflection of him; that people will judge his character by what they see on a person's Timeline both today and in the future. Encourage him not to post anything he doesn't want his grandma, teachers, or a prospective employer to see.

  Teens also need to be careful about sharing photos of themselves, information about where they go to school and their daily activities and routines, and weekend and vacation plans to travel away from home with family, all of which can be used to harm the teen or teen's family in some way.

- Warn your child of phishing scams, as explained in Chapter 2. The two biggies are these: 1) Don't share your password with anyone; and 2) Accept friend requests only from people you know and trust.

- Encourage your teenager to block anyone who harasses her or her friends online and report any incidents of bad behavior to Facebook. Also let your teenager know that you're always available to listen if she is concerned about what somebody posted or what someone she met on Facebook might do.

POKE

Becoming friends with your child doesn't mean you'll have visual access to everything they do on Facebook. Facebook Chat and Messages are private, so unless you're standing over your child's shoulder at all times, you won't be able to see what's contained in their private messages to others on Facebook.

Some experts suggest that as a condition for using Facebook, parents obtain their teenager's account password. Although this might be good advice for some, savvy teens can always create two accounts— one to show Mom and Dad how good they are and another account outside the gaze of Mom and Dad that they use to interact with their friends. Building a relationship of mutual trust and respect is usually a more effective approach for establishing and maintaining open lines of communication that lead to safe practices on Facebook.

If you're concerned about the company your teenager keeps on Facebook and other social networking venues, consider using a service such as SocialShield to help monitor your teen's online activities. SocialShield (www.socialshield.com), for example, can keep track of your teenager's and his or her friends' activities and email you warnings when certain activities might be a cause for concern. Plenty of other services and software are available for monitoring computer usage and social networking activity, including Social Guard by ZoneAlarm (www.zonealarm.com).

FRIEND-LY ADVICE

Many homes have access to wireless internet through a router, and most routers have some sort of parental controls built in. In most cases, you can block access for certain hours of each day, block access to specific sites, and have the router keep a log of sites that have been visited from each computer on the network. Find out how to log in to your router's control panel and explore its features. While you're there, you might want to change the router's password to something your teenager is less likely to guess or find in the router manual next to your computer.

For additional guidance on how to keep your children safe on Facebook, check out Facebook's Help system. Open the **Account** menu at the far right of the blue bar at the top of any Facebook page (the button with the down arrow on it), click **Help**, click **Go to Help Center**, and click **Safety Center** for links to several topics about Facebook safety. The Safety Center also has a section just for teens.

Providing Supervision as a Teacher or Caregiver

Teachers, youth-group leaders, and other adults often take on the supervisory role when parents are not present. As the responsible adult, the first step to take is to review or establish a social networking policy that delineates the use of social networking in and outside the classroom or group. In Chapter 15, we discuss how to go about drafting a social networking policy for business use, which provides some guidance that's useful for schools and other organizations, as well.

In addition to following policy, here are some tips for teachers and others who take on a supervisory role for safely incorporating Facebook in the program:

- Create a Facebook page or closed group to keep teens and their parents informed. In a classroom situation, you can use a Facebook Group to distribute homework and permission slips, share photos and videos of field trips and classroom activities, share student art, and keep everyone posted about upcoming events. With a Facebook page, you don't have to friend parents or their children, but pages are public, so outsiders can Like the page and receive updates, which might not be the best solution.

- If you friend students or parents, be particularly careful about what you post and whom you choose to share it with. Review your privacy settings, as explained in Chapter 2, and use friend lists, as explained in Chapter 4, to keep your social contact separate from the students and parents you friend.

- Report any inappropriate content you notice, and block any individuals who engage in unacceptable behavior.

Interpreting Teenspeak: Social Networking Acronyms

Acronyms are standard fare on Facebook, Twitter, and other social networking venues. You're probably aware that *LOL* stands for *Laughing Out Loud* and perhaps that *BRB* is short for *Be Right Back*. Certain acronyms commonly used among teenagers might serve as red flags, as listed in Table 11-1.

Table 11-1 Social networking acronyms that parents and teachers should know

Acronym	Stands for
182	I Hate You
5	Wait a few minutes, parents are around
55	Okay to talk, parents are gone
AITR	Adult In The Room
ASLRP	Age? Sex? Location? Race? Picture?
BIH	Burn In Hell
BYTABM	Beat You To A Bloody Mess
CD9	Parents are around

Acronym	Stands for
CRAFT	Can't Recall A F***ing Thing
D46?	Down For Sex?
DIAH	Die In A Hole
F2F	Face To Face meeting
FML	F*** My Life
FOAD	F*** Off And Die
FUD	Fear Uncertainty Doubt
GKY	Go Kill Yourself
GNOC	Get Naked On Camera
GTFO	Get The F*** Out
HSWM	Have Sex With Me
IDGAF	I Don't Give A F***
IHML	I Hate My Life
IHTFP	I Hate This F***ing Place
LMA	Leave Me Alone
MIRL	Meet In Real Life
NIFOC	Naked In Front Of Computer
OTH	Off The Hook (over the top, wild, or hot)
P911	Parent emergency
PHAT	Pretty Hot And Tempting
PHM	Please Help Me
POS	Parent Over Shoulder
S2R	Send To Receive (photo)
STFU	Shut The F*** Up
STR8	Straight (sexual orientation and free of drugs/alcohol)
Sugarpic	Suggestive or erotic picture of self
TDTM	Talk Dirty To Me
UDI	Unidentified Drinking Injury
W2M	Want To Meet?
WTGP	Want To Go Private?

For more chat and social networking abbreviations, acronyms, and codes, visit www.netlingo.com.

The Least You Need to Know

- Join Facebook if you haven't already, get a feel for how it works, and be sure to friend your child.

- Don't let a child under the age of 13 years use Facebook —it's against the Facebook terms of service.

- If you're a parent, discuss Facebook and online safety issues with your teenager. Act dumb. Ask lots of questions.

- Be aware that information shared in Messages and Chat is private and only visible to your child.

- Encourage teenagers to share with care—innocent information in the wrong hands can be harmful.

- For closer monitoring of a teen's activities on Facebook, check into a program like Social Shield.

Harnessing the Power of Facebook Apps

Without its apps (applications), Facebook is the stripped-down model of a social-networking utility. All you'd have left is the Timeline, News Feed, and some Profile data. Add in Facebook's core apps, and you get the fully loaded model, complete with Photos, Videos, Groups, Events, Messages, and Chat. All of these features are Facebook apps, which act sort of like plugins to make Facebook so feature-rich.

But there's more. Facebook and third-party developers provide even more apps to enhance Facebook, including apps to play games, use Facebook on your smartphone, share lists of your favorite books or movies, check your horoscope, send online greeting cards, and even get special deals from merchants when you "check in" to the business's Facebook Place using your smartphone. In this part, we reveal all you need to know to app up.

Exploring Facebook Apps

In This Chapter

- Recognizing a Facebook app when you meet one
- Exploring Facebook's massive apps collection
- Dealing with app security and privacy issues
- Tweaking your Apps menu and bookmarks for easy app access
- Adjusting your Facebook app settings
- Dealing with app security and privacy issues

Bet you didn't realize it, but you've already been using Facebook apps (applications). Photos, Video, Groups, Events, and Chat—they're all apps. These apps function as plugins for Facebook—accessories that enhance your experience. They add features that aren't part of the core Facebook experience (although a few select apps, like Photos and Chat, are part of the core experience).

In this chapter, we introduce you to app basics, reveal where you can find thousands of apps on Facebook, and show you how to gain quicker access to the apps you use.

Grasping the Basics of Facebook Apps

Facebook apps can help you do all sorts of things—from playing games to tracking birthdays and anniversaries and sharing movie reviews with friends. Facebook gives you access to thousands of apps, some its own creations but mostly those created by third-party developers. Later in this chapter, we show you how to search for specific apps and browse through Facebook's ever-growing collection of apps by category.

Fortunately, you have complete control over which apps you use. You can approve an app, block an app, or edit an app to control how it accesses and uses your information. If a friend invites you to use an app, you're entirely free to accept or reject the invitation.

In the following sections, we show you how to browse Facebook's complete collection of apps and search for specific apps. We also explain some of the security and privacy issues surrounding apps and how to deal with them.

Digging Up More Apps

You're likely to discover plenty of apps through referrals as your friends recommend and invite you to use popular apps, especially games. If that doesn't satisfy your appetite, you can explore Facebook to gather more fun and useful apps.

Facebook has a well-stocked library of apps, which you can browse or search at any time. One way to browse for apps is to head to the Timeline Apps page at www.facebook.com/about/timeline/apps and click the desired category in the Add apps to your timeline today section.

Another way to browse Facebook apps is through the Apps and Games dashboard. Head to your Home page, and click **Apps and Games** in the left column. The Apps and Games dashboard contains several sections to help you find apps and games that are likely to interest you, including Invites from friends, Requests from friends, Apps and Games, Game Promotions, and Discover New Games.

Go to www.facebook.com/about/timeline/apps

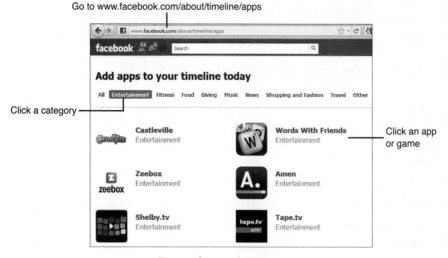

Browse for apps by category.

Click Apps and Games

The Apps and Games dashboard.

Scroll down to the **Apps and Games** section and click one of the following options to specify the types of Facebook apps you want to browse:

- **Recommended Games:** Popular games that you're likely to find your friends playing.

- **Friends Using:** Games and other Facebook apps that your friends have used recently.

- **Recommended Apps:** Popular Facebook apps, not including games, that you're likely to find your friends using.

- **Newest:** Current games and Facebook apps.

To search for an app, click in the **Search** box (in the top menu), type one or two words to describe the type of app you're looking for, click **See more results for <whatever you typed>**, and click **Apps** in the left column.

If more than 10 apps matched your description, you find a See More Results link below the search results, which you can click on to see more apps that match your search word or phrase.

Search for an app

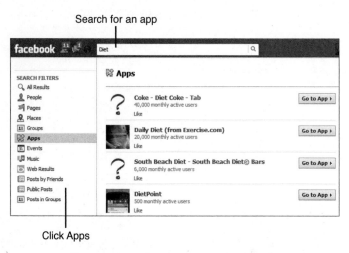

Click Apps

You can search for specific apps or types of apps.

Authorizing Apps

To use an app, you have to authorize it, giving it permission to access some of your data and perhaps post content to your Timeline or News Feed. To obtain a little background information about an app, click its link wherever you happen to see it. The app's About page appears, displaying a brief description of the app, a list of information the app will receive, and usually a statement indicating that the app may post on your behalf. You can usually choose a privacy setting to specify who can see what the app posts on your behalf. You can then click a button to start playing the game or using the app or to cancel.

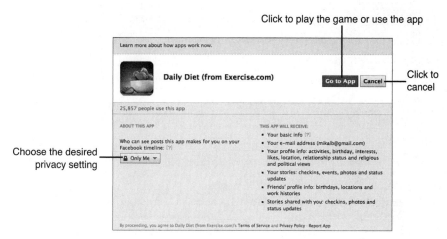

Click to play the game or use the app

Click to cancel

Choose the desired privacy setting

Check out an app before authorizing it.

When you authorize an app, Facebook creates a bookmark for it; bookmarked apps appear in the left menu in a separate section designated for your apps (just above the Friends section the last we checked).

POKE

Facebook automatically rearranges your bookmarked apps as you use them, listing the apps you use most frequently first.

Visiting a Game's or App's Fan Page

To find out more about a game or app, visit its page. Start typing its name in the **Search** box and then click the entry below Pages that has the most "Likes" (usually the topmost entry below Pages). If the game or app has thousands (or millions) of Likes, it's probably something you can trust.

On a fan page, you can choose to Like the game or app, start using it, block it, report it, and more.

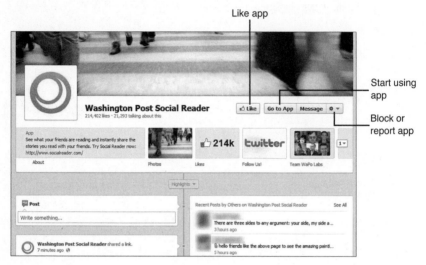

Visit a game's or app's Fan page to find out more about it.

Responding to an App Invitation or Request

When you receive an app or game invitation or request, the question for you is whether to authorize the app. If a friend has invited you to play a game or try an app, you can click **Play Now** or **Try Now** to start playing the game or using the app right away. All you need to do is give the game or app permission to access certain account information. To respond to a request, click the **Accept** button and then authorize the game or app or click the **X** button to cancel the request.

You'll also see games and apps popping up on your News Feed or Ticker, as a subtle invitation to participate. Assuming your friend hasn't disabled the News Feed notifications for apps, whenever he uses an app, a status update might appear in your News Feed and Ticker indicating something related to your friend's interaction with the app. At the end of the post, you find the usual links to comment on the update or Like it, along with another link to start using the app or some feature of it. Click the link to find out more about the app. Facebook displays some information about the app along with options to use the app or cancel.

Game and app invitations

You can accept or cancel an app request.

Editing and Removing Apps

Depending on the app you authorize, Facebook gives you some freedom to tweak the app's settings. For example, you can hide the Photos tab in your Profile, change the tab's privacy settings to limit access to it, or change the app's permissions to grant or revoke special privileges, such as sending you messages or posting updates to your Timeline.

To edit an app's settings:

1. Open the **Account** menu (top right) and click **Privacy Settings**.

2. Near the bottom of the page, below Apps and Websites, click **Edit Settings**.

3. Next to Apps you use, click the **Edit Settings** button. This displays a list of apps you recently used.

4. Next to the app whose settings you want to adjust, click **Edit**. Settings appear for controlling the app's accessibility and permissions. These settings vary depending on the app; for example, you may be able to click **X** next to an option that enables the app to post updates to your Timeline.

5. Enter your preferences, and then click the **Close** button.

The app itself might offer additional settings via its interface. Look for an option labeled Settings or Profile Settings when you're using the app.

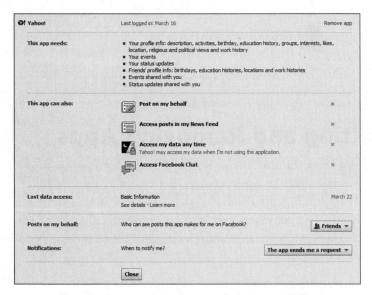

You can edit an app's settings to adjust its accessibility and permissions.

Some apps don't allow edits; however, you can remove any app you've added. To remove an app:

1. Open the **Account** menu (top right) and click **Privacy Settings**.

2. Near the bottom of the page, below Apps and Websites, click **Edit Settings**.

3. Next to Apps you use, click the **Edit Settings** button. Next to the app you want to remove, click the **X** button.

You also have the option to turn off all apps. Open the **Account** menu (top right) and click **Privacy Settings**. Near the bottom of the page, below Apps and Websites, click **Edit Settings**. Near the bottom of the Apps you use section, click **Turn off all apps**. With all apps turned off, you no longer need to be concerned about information you or your friends choose to share with apps, because no app can access your information.

FRIEND-LY ADVICE

If you're in the process of viewing or editing an app's settings, you can remove the app by clicking the **Remove app** link (to the upper-right corner of the app's settings).

While you're at it, check out some of the other settings on the Privacy Settings page for Apps, Games, and Websites. Open the **Account** menu (top right) and click **Privacy Settings**. Near the bottom of the page, below Apps and Websites, click **Edit Settings**. Click the **Edit Settings** button next to any of the following options to check the existing settings:

- **How people bring your info into the apps they use:** You can specify the type of information, if any, that apps can access, including your bio, birthday, family relationships, photos, education and work, interests, and app activity.

- **Instant personalization:** Facebook has teamed up with several websites, including Bing, TripAdvisor, Yelp, and Rotten Tomatoes, to enable those sites to tailor their content to better serve your interests. You can disable instant personalization for these partner websites.

- **Public search:** With Public Search enabled, people who search for you on sites like Google and Bing may see some of your Timeline information. You can disable Public Search to prevent your Timeline information from being indexed by search engines.

The Least You Need to Know

- To browse Facebook's games and apps, go to www. facebook.com/about/timeline/apps or click **Apps and Games** in the left column.

- To search for apps, click in the **Search** box (top menu), type your search word or phrase, click **See more results for <whatever you typed>**, and then click **Apps** (in the left menu).

- To access one of your apps, click its bookmark (left menu) or click **Apps** (in the left column) and then select the app from your Apps page.

- To find the Fan page for a game or app, type its name in the Search box, and then click the topmost entry below Pages.

- To tweak an app's settings, open the Account menu (upper-right corner), click **Privacy Settings**, scroll down below Apps and Websites, click **Edit Settings**, click **Edit Settings** (next to Apps you use), click **Edit** next to the app you want to edit, and use the resulting options to enter your preferences.

Playing Games with Friends and Strangers

In This Chapter

- Checking out the top games on Facebook
- Finding even more games to play
- Convincing friends to join in the fun
- Making new friends through games

A lot of people waste … er … *spend* a lot of time on Facebook playing all sorts of games, voting in polls, and taking personality tests like "Which flower represents you?" and "Which dead rock star are you?"

If you enjoy sharing in the revelry, this chapter introduces you to some of the most popular games and other distractions on Facebook, shows you how to find even more games and add them to your list of favorites, and explains how to engage others in a friendly game of whatever it is you enjoy playing. Games can be a great way to meet new friends.

Oh, the Games People Play!

Social games on Facebook are all the rage, but different games appeal to different people. In addition, the popularity of certain games tends to rise and fall. When poker was all the rage, Texas Hold'Em Poker was one of the most popular games on Facebook, followed closely by Mafia Wars. After some time, however, people began leaving the card table for FarmVille, where they could manage their own virtual farms in cyberspace.

In the following list, you get to sample the games that made the top-10 list while we were writing the book. We'd wager that by the time you read this, some of these games won't make the cut, and new games will have risen to the top, but these top popular options give you a pretty good feel for the cross-section of social games available on Facebook:

1. **CityVille:** In CityVille, you build a city from the ground up by growing crops and supplying produce to stores and restaurants. As your city grows, you build houses, collect rent, create businesses, expand into other cities with franchise operations, erect community buildings, exchange goods, and manage finances in the hopes of becoming Mayor of your fair city.

2. **Texas Hold'Em Poker:** Zynga's popular poker game enables you to ante up with your friends and engage in one of the classic games of all time … Texas style. You start each day with a small stack of chips plus any winnings you have accumulated from previous games. If you have a credit card handy, you can purchase more chips, or you can sign up for offers from companies to receive free chips. Unfortunately, you can't cash out that $5 million you won the night before.

3. **Hidden Chronicles:** In this hidden-object game by Zynga, your goal is to unlock the secrets of Ramsey Manor by uncovering concealed objects, solving puzzles, and finding clues. Play with friends by leaving them helpful gifts or sending a challenge to see which friend can find the most clues in a given scene.

4. **Draw Something:** Draw Something is sort of like an online version of Pictionary. You get a word to illustrate, and as you draw your illustration, your friends or other players guess the word you're trying to illustrate. Draw Something enables you to compete against others or play cooperatively with friends.

5. **FarmVille:** In FarmVille, you till the soil, plant seeds and trees, harvest cash crops, build farmhouses and barns, milk cows, decorate, expand your farm, and even invest in farm machinery to make your job easier. Invite your Facebook

friends to settle on neighboring farmland, and you can help them with their farms to earn extra cash. If you get serious about this farming thing, you can pay real cash to buy game money that'll help you build your farm faster.

6. **CastleVille:** CastleVille invites you to "build a castle, rule your kingdom, and get happy." Several colorful characters populate CastleVille, including the fair maiden, Yvette; Tom, the dragon slayer; George, the miner; Sonya, the gold digger pirate; and Raphael, the Don Juan of the Dark Ages. As you play CastleVille, you get to meet these characters and more, and team up with your Facebook friends to build a fantastic kingdom and achieve a happy ending.

7. **Words with Friends:** This popular word game is essentially an online version of Scrabble. At the start of the game, you receive seven letter tiles. You and other players take turns placing your letter tiles on a board to create words and score points. If you don't like your tiles, you can use a turn to exchange them. While waiting for a friend to play, you can send the friend a message, start a game with another friend, or do something else.

8. **Angry Birds:** Angry Birds is a story of revenge. After pigs eat their eggs, the Angry Birds unleash their fury by destroying the pigs' fortified castles … with the pigs inside them. Destroying castles requires logic, skill, and brute force. Some knowledge of physics is also useful.

9. **Diamond Dash:** In this pattern-matching game, you try to eliminate as many blocks of same-color gems as possible in the course of 60 seconds. If you run out of lives, just ask your friends for more lives.

10. **The Sims Social:** The Sims is a popular computer game that has transitioned to Facebook. You create your own unique characters, build your dream home, make friends and enemies, share a first kiss, play pranks to stir up trouble, and much more. In the Facebook version, you can do all this and more with your friends.

Plant and harvest virtual crops in FarmVille.

Finding Games on Facebook

Tracking down games on Facebook is as easy as tracking down apps, as explained in Chapter 12. In fact, games are apps. Although you can use the Search box in the top menu to perform a broad search for games, you're usually better off browsing Facebook's collection. To start browsing, head to your Home page and click **Apps and Games** (in the left menu). This takes you to the Apps and Games dashboard, which is divided into several sections, including Apps and Games and Discover New Games.

Under Apps and Games, click **Recommended Games** to view some of the most popular Facebook games. In the left menu, below Apps and Games, click **Friend Activity** to see Facebook games that your friends have recently played and apps they've used.

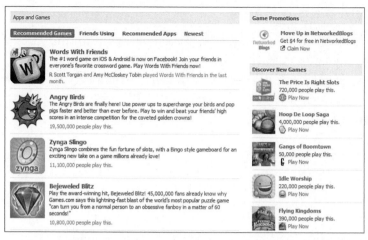

Browse the Apps and Games dashboard to find games.

Let's Play Already!

Every game is unique, so providing instructions on how to play each one would be ridiculous. All we have room to cover are the basics—launching the game, inviting friends to play, and responding to invitations from friends.

POKE

Unfortunately, game developers typically provide little or no guidance for new players to get up and running. You pretty much have to start playing and hope that on-the-job training is sufficient. You might be able to pick up a little guidance on the game's page. Type the game's name in the **Search** box and look for entries below Pages. If you have friends who play the game, you can consult them. You can also search the web for instructions—sometimes players post basic instructions on sites such as eHow.com or the game's developer offers a beginner's guide.

Launching a Game

Whenever you authorize a game, Facebook adds it to your Apps page and bookmarks it, so a link to the game appears in the left menu. When you're ready to play, click the game's bookmark or click **APPS** (left menu) and then click the game you want to play.

To play a game, click its name in the left menu or on the Apps page.

Encouraging Your Friends to Play

The main purpose of social games is to socialize, so almost every game on Facebook is geared to engage friends in the fun. FarmVille, for example, constantly encourages players to spread the word and invite friends to play. The invitation can be something soft, such as posting a story, or something more direct, like asking your friends to help you find a home for the new kitten that just wandered onto your property. You can also invite friends at any time by clicking **Invite Friends**. If your friends are already FarmVille players, click **Add Neighbors** to make them your neighbors.

However you choose to invite friends to play, an Invite Friends page pops up, prompting you to select from your list of friends.

Click the friends you want to invite and click the button to send your invitation(s).

You can invite friends to join in the fun.

 WHOA!

Avoid the temptation to invite all of your friends to play the cool new game you just discovered. Invite only those friends you know enjoy playing games, and from that subset, select only the friends you strongly feel will enjoy playing *this* game. Invite the wrong person too many times, and she's likely to either block your future invitations or unfriend you.

Making New Friends Through Games

If you're having trouble finding friends to play your favorite game with you, consider joining a group devoted to the game. Check out Chapter 9 to learn more about groups and how to find and join groups. You're likely to find several groups packed with people eager to meet new players. In addition, your new friends can help bring you up to speed on the game and provide useful tips.

To find a group for a game, click in the **Search** box (top menu), type the name of the game, click **See more results for <game>**, and click **Groups** (left menu).

Responding to a Friend's Request to Play

If someone sends you an invitation to play a game, you should see a notification for it in the blue bar at the top. Click **Apps and Games** in the left column to access the Apps and Games dashboard. You can then click the game's name to find out more about it, click **Play Now** to accept the invitation, or click **X** to hide the invitation.

If you hide the invitation, Facebook gives you two more options. You can block the game, so you never receive invitations from anyone to play this particular game, or you can ignore all requests from the person who sent you the invitation, so you never receive another invitation from this person to play a game or use an app. (You can undo this at any time by adjusting your privacy settings, as explained in Chapter 2.)

The Least You Need to Know

- Facebook games are social games, designed for group interaction.
- Some of the more popular Facebook games include CityVille, Texas Hold'Em Poker, Hidden Chronicles, and Draw Something.
- To find games, head to your Home page and click **Apps and Games** (in the left menu).
- After authorizing a game, you can find a bookmark for it in the left menu or click **APPS** in the left menu to view all of your apps and games.
- Be selective when inviting friends to play games. Not all of your friends will appreciate receiving game invitations.

Facebooking with Your Mobile Phone or Device

In This Chapter

- Using a smartphone app to access Facebook
- Setting up Facebook Mobile on your phone
- Receiving and sending status updates remotely
- Uploading digital photos and video clips from your phone
- Checking in and redeeming offers

When you leave your home or office or wherever you usually spend time on Facebook, you don't have to leave your friends behind. In fact, you might find that using Facebook on your mobile phone or mobile device is actually more useful and convenient than on your laptop or desktop computer. Think about it; many of today's cell phones have built-in photo, video, and texting capabilities, which is exactly why most people use Facebook—to share photos, status updates, and videos. Why wait until you're in front of your computer when you can do all of that and more right from your mobile device?

Assuming you have a cell phone, iPhone, iPad, Android device, BlackBerry, Palm, or other such wireless gadget, you can update your status, view and upload photos and videos, check your Facebook messages, check in at businesses and locations you visit, redeem Offers, and more. This chapter takes you on the road with your mobile device and shows you how to join the more-than-450 million people who access Facebook using their mobile devices.

Accessing Facebook with a Smartphone App

For the majority of us who use a smartphone (think iPhone, BlackBerry, Palm, Android device, and so on), the Facebook experience is only as good as the smartphone's app. And although we all want the same user experience and interface we enjoy on our desktop computers to appear on our smartphone, well ... that just isn't possible. Aside from the fact that phone screens are at best half the size of the smallest desktop monitor or power user's laptop screen, there's the whole issue of bandwidth and connectivity, both of which dictate that the user experience on a mobile device is going to be, well, different.

Whether you use an iPhone, iPad, Android, or nearly any other type of mobile device, device-specific apps are available for you to connect with and enjoy Facebook from the palm of your hand. Each device has app stores where you can download your device's Facebook app. To get started, visit the app store associated with your mobile phone or device and search for "Facebook." Once you find your device-specific app, follow the on-screen instructions for downloading the app to your phone.

> **FRIEND-LY ADVICE**
>
> Although many of today's smartphones come with a preinstalled Facebook app, some might not. Head to www.facebook.com/mobile to see whether Facebook has the app you need. iPhone users can access the Apple App Store via their phone or iTunes on a desktop or laptop computer. BlackBerry's app store can be found at www.blackberry.com. If your phone runs the Android operating system, visit play.google.com/store for your phone's Facebook app.

Setting Up Facebook Mobile

If you're old school and prefer to skip using an app to access Facebook, the first thing you need to do is log in to your Facebook account using your computer and enter **Mobile** in the Search box, or visit www.facebook.com/mobile. At the bottom of the page, click **Edit Mobile Settings**.

FRIEND-LY ADVICE

Make sure your cell phone is web-enabled. If you can browse the World Wide Web and send and receive text messages using your phone, you're all set. If, however, your cell phone isn't web-enabled or set up to send and receive text messages, you'll need to consult your wireless carrier about switching to a phone that enables you to use Facebook.

Clicking on the **Edit Mobile Settings** link brings you to the Mobile tab of your Account Settings, where you can register your mobile phone for Facebook Text Messages, which include status updates, messages, and more.

Click **+ Add a Phone** and follow the on-screen prompts to complete the setup. Facebook sends a confirmation code to your smartphone that you need to enter into Facebook to confirm that you're the rightful owner of the phone registered to that number.

That's it. Your mobile phone is now activated to use Facebook Mobile, and you're ready to roll. Now you're all set to start receiving status updates. To designate a friend or page you want to receive status updates from via your mobile phone, visit the **Mobile** tab under **Account Settings**, and in the **Notifications** section, enter the name of the friend or page under **You will receive text notifications whenever the following friends update their status message**. (For more about Facebook pages, see Chapter 16.)

Of course, Facebook Mobile enables you to do more than simply receive status updates. You can now post status updates, share photos and videos, send and receive Facebook messages, add a friend by name or phone number, and use third-party applications that enhance your Facebook experience and productivity. Keep reading to tap the full potential of Facebook Mobile.

WHOA!

Although Facebook doesn't charge for status updates, and messages, your mobile service provider does. Check your mobile rate plan before signing up to send messages and receive all your friends' status updates as text messages on your phone. As you see later in this chapter, if you're not on one of those all-inclusive plans, you might be better off using Facebook via your phone's web browser, if it's equipped with one.

Texting to Facebook

After you've activated your phone to send and receive Facebook status updates and messages, performing those tasks is as easy as texting. In fact, at this stage, interfacing with Facebook is all about texting, as we explain in the following sections. (And if you stop and think about it, posting status updates when you're out and about, when you're experiencing life and have more to say or sitting around twiddling your thumbs in a waiting room or airport, makes a lot more sense, too.) Most Facebook users don't post status updates only when they're sitting in front of their computers. We can't tell you how many times we've found the need—okay, it's really more of a *desire* than a need—to post status updates on the road, in the passenger seat of the car, at a restaurant waiting for a friend, sitting in the airport, or at a game where the most amazing thing just happened.

Having the flexibility to share interesting news, opinions, and observations with our Facebook friends whenever and wherever the spirit moves us is a real treat. Some business owners and leaders have come to consider it a necessity. In the following sections, we show you how to use Facebook Mobile to access Facebook's most popular features when you're away from your computer.

Posting Status Updates

Once you've authorized your cell phone for Facebook Mobile, posting status updates from your phone is as simple as sending an SMS (short message service) to 32665 (FBOOK). Said differently, text a message—for example, "I'm reading *The Complete Idiot's Guide to Facebook*; you should, too!"—from your Facebook-enabled cell phone to 32665 and it will show up in your Facebook account as a status update.

But wait, there's more.

Texting Facebook Commands

Now that your phone is set up to send and receive messages from Facebook, you can do any of the following activities:

- **Send a message to a Facebook friend:** Text **msg** followed by your friend's name followed by your message to 32665, and your text shows up in your friend's Inbox on Facebook. For example, "msg joseph kraynak running 45 min late."

- **Subscribe or unsubscribe to a Facebook member's updates:** Text **subscribe jane doe** to 32665 to receive status updates that the person posts. Text **unsubscribe jane doe** to 32665 to stop receiving the person's posts.

- **Stop or start SMS:** Text **stop** to 32665 to stop Facebook Mobile or text **on** to 32665 to restart it.

- **Get help:** Text **help** to 32665 to get general help with using Facebook Mobile or text **photos** for help with uploading photos.

- **Search for a friend's Facebook details:** Text **search [name]** to 32665, and you receive a text message from Facebook containing your friend's Facebook data, which usually includes at least a phone number and email address. For example, "search Mikal Belicove" will result in receiving a message with Mikal's publicly available information on Facebook (assuming he's your friend).

- **Post a note on Facebook:** Text **note** followed by your note's content to 32665 and your note appears on Facebook and in your News Feed.

- **Post a message on a friend's Timeline or Wall:** Text **wall** followed by your friend's name followed by your post to 32665, and your message appears on your friend's Facebook Timeline or Wall. For example, "wall Mikal Belicove Really enjoying *The Complete Idiot's Guide to Facebook*. Nicely done!"

- **Send a friend request:** Text **add** followed by your future Facebook friend's name to 32665 to send a friend request. For example, text "add Mikal Belicove" to send Mikal a friend request.

- **Become a fan:** Text **fan** followed by the name of the Facebook fan page to 32665 to instantly become a fan of a specific page on Facebook. For example, text "fan Idiot Book" to become a fan of our official page for the book.

Taking Facebook Mobile Web on the Road

If your cell phone can access the internet and has a web browser, check out m.facebook.com from your phone's browser. Here you find Facebook Mobile Web, a version of Facebook that's optimized for cell phones with web browser capabilities.

Facebook Mobile Web might look different depending on the mobile device and browser you're using to access it. In most cases, a menu button displays in the upper-right corner of the screen. Click the button to display a menu that looks similar to the menu that displays in the left column when you're using the nonmobile version of Facebook.

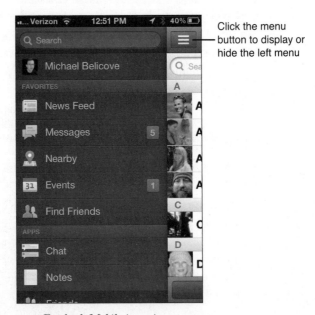

Click the menu button to display or hide the left menu

Facebook Mobile in action.

In other cases, you might have a menu bar across the top of the browser followed by Facebook's Publisher and your News Feed.

Uploading Photos and Videos from Your Phone

With a photo- or video-enabled cell phone, you no longer need to download photos or videos to your home computer or laptop and then go through the steps outlined in Chapters 7 and 8 to upload them to Facebook. With Facebook Mobile, you simply shoot your photos and videos on your phone and upload them directly to Facebook Mobile. The process varies depending on your phone and configuration.

In most cases, you can go to m.facebook.com and click the **Photo** button at the top of your Profile or Timeline, News Feed, friend's Profile or Timeline, or any groups you're in, and then follow the on-screen prompts to choose the photo you want to upload and complete the process.

Upload a photo to Facebook.

If you're using an iPhone or iPad, tap the photo button, choose an existing photo or take a photo, tag the photo and tap **Next**, and follow the on-screen prompts to complete the upload.

You can also upload photos and videos by sending them via email to your personal publishing address. To find out what that address is, go to m.facebook.com, tap the menu button (upper-left corner), tap **Photos** (left menu), and tap **Upload Photos**. Below Upload via Email is your personal publishing address.

> **FRIEND-LY ADVICE**
>
> The steps for accessing your personal publishing address vary depending on the browser you're using, but you can usually find it by poking around in the photo upload areas.

When you upload via email, whatever you type into your message's subject line automatically becomes the title of the video or the caption of the photo you're uploading.

After you've uploaded your photos or videos to Facebook, the uploaded items are automatically posted to your Profile. Photos show up in your Mobile Uploads album, which is accessible via your Photos box, and video files are stored on your Video box. We recommend editing uploaded photos and videos the next time you log in to Facebook, because the only content set for Mobile Uploads is the caption for photos and title for videos. See Chapter 7 for more on editing photos and Chapter 8 for information on editing videos.

Checking In on Facebook

When you're on the go, you might want to let your friends know where you are and what you're doing … and find out where they are and what they're doing. That's possible by using the Check In and Nearby features—location-based options that let you check in wherever you happen to be and tag any Facebook friends you're with, as well as view friends when they're nearby.

To start using the Check In feature, you need a smartphone (such as iPhone, Android, or BlackBerry) equipped with its up-to-date Facebook app. Another option is to access the Check In feature through your mobile device's web browser by going to m.facebook. com. You must be using a browser that supports HTML5 and geolocation. (You can also use the Check In feature from a portable computer or tablet like the iPad.)

After logging in using your mobile device's Facebook app, tap the menu button (upper-left corner) and tap **Nearby**. On the resulting page, you see where your friends have recently checked in and any of your own recent check-ins. You can tap or click a friend's check-in to view additional details about it, any comments that others have posted about it, and any Likes it has garnered. In addition, you can choose to check in, as explained next.

After reaching a physical location, you can check in to let Facebook know where you are. Click the **Check In** button. The first time you choose to check in, you'll probably be prompted by Facebook or your browser to allow Facebook to access your geographical location. Follow the on-screen prompts to grant or deny permission. Of course, if you deny permission, you won't be able to check in.

Assuming you've given Facebook permission to access your geographical location, you're prompted to specify your location. Facebook might have some suggestions, based on data collected from your mobile device and browser, or you might be presented with a Search box you can use to enter details about your location. Follow the on-screen prompts to specify your location.

After you choose your location, Facebook's Publisher appears, enabling you to post an update. Click in the **What's on your mind?** box and type a description of what you're doing or thinking. You can also choose to tag friends you're with, attach a photo, and choose the people you want to share this post with. When you're done, tap or click **Share**.

Check in to share your location with others.

If you're in the vicinity of a restaurant or store you frequent that has a Facebook page, consider pulling up its page for offers and Check-in Deals. Click the **Check-in Deal** for instructions on how to redeem it. You usually redeem a Deal by showing it on your mobile device's screen to the store clerk or server.

> **FRIEND-LY ADVICE**
>
> If you want to use Facebook as a locations-based marketing tool for your business, check out Chapter 16, where you learn about Facebook pages and how to offer Check-in Deals to your page's followers.

Taking Advantage of Offers

Now you have an even better reason for using Facebook on your mobile device. At the time of writing this edition of the book, Facebook was beta-testing Offers, a new way for businesses to provide value to people and customers who Like them on Facebook.

Offers enables businesses, brands, and other Facebook page owners to, well, "offer" discounts and other offers to fans. For businesses, making an Offer is as simple as posting a Status Update. Once an Offer is posted to a business's Timeline and it shows up in the News Feed, Facebook users can take advantage of it by clicking the **Claim** button beneath the offer.

Businesses create Offers to attract more customers, retain existing customers, and generate sales without the hassle of printed coupons. You simply pull up the Offer on your mobile display and show it to the person who's serving you.

If you own a business and want to create Offers, skip to Chapter 18 to learn how.

The Least You Need to Know

- Most smartphones have a Facebook app that makes accessing the site fun and easy. Visit your phone's app store to find the Facebook app best suited for your phone.
- To set up Facebook Mobile for your cell phone, head to www.facebook.com/mobile, click **Edit Settings**, and follow the on-screen instructions.
- To post a status update from your cell phone, send a text message to 32665 (FBOOK).
- To post a message on a friend's Timeline or Wall, text **wall** followed by your friend's name followed by your Timeline or Wall post to 32665.
- To obtain a personalized Facebook email address for mobile uploads, go to www.facebook.com/mobile.
- To Check In at a particular location, log in to Facebook using your mobile phone's Facebook app or browser and click the **Check In button**.

Utilizing Facebook for Businesses and Organizations

Doing business or promoting a nonprofit on Facebook is sort of like selling raffle tickets at a family reunion. People gather on Facebook to socialize, not to buy stuff, and they don't appreciate being blasted with sales pitches or promotions. Yet most Facebook users expect businesses and organizations to have a presence in the community and provide something engaging and beneficial—typically valuable, relevant information and maybe special offers.

In this part, we try to sell you on the idea of doing business or establishing a presence for your organization on Facebook. If you're looking to do business on Facebook, you'll discover how to use Facebook to boost sales, increase customer retention, and attract new customers without turning off the people you're trying to impress. If you're running an organization, you'll discover how to use Facebook to keep members engaged and informed and grow your ranks.

Promoting Your Business or Organization

In This Chapter

- Recognizing the business potential of Facebook
- Incorporating Facebook advertising in your marketing campaign
- Getting customers involved with groups
- Avoiding the most common pitfalls

Selling effectively in a social setting requires a huge paradigm shift from traditional marketing, advertising, and sales. On Facebook and other social-networking sites, establishing credibility and trust and building relationships take precedence over making a sale. Companies and brands that succeed are rewarded through positive word-of-mouth advertising and referrals. Those who ruffle the feathers of too many Facebook members feel their wrath as the negative publicity spreads almost instantly.

In this chapter, we make the case for implementing Facebook in your marketing and engagement efforts, introduce you to features designed specifically for these purposes, and provide tips on how to market and engage most effectively on Facebook.

The Business Case for Facebook

If we told you 900,000,000+ people were happily gathered in one central location online—many of whom are your customers and prospective customers—and that the majority of them expect to see your business or brand there, wouldn't you want to be there, too? In a nutshell, that's the case for marketing your business or brand on Facebook. With hundreds of millions of consumers using this one über–social networking utility to connect with friends and interact with others around topics that interest them, your business has a tremendous opportunity to gain powerful access to the very people who fill your coffers.

Unlike banner, email, and pay-per-click advertising (push-marketing tactics, in which you push your message to the masses and wait for a direct response), setting up shop for your business on Facebook is a highly effective *pull* strategy. When done correctly, it enables you to engage with your customers—and engagement is what Facebook is all about.

With engagement comes the possibility of word-of-mouth advertising, which, of course, is nothing new. What is new is that the internet has become the breeding ground for participation, and along with it, the placement and distribution of user-generated content—and not just the stuff related to the funny sound your cat just made. Users participate by writing about businesses and products, asking and answering questions, posting and reading reviews, sharing rip-off stories about bad experiences they've had with certain companies, and often going so far as to sing the praises of top-notch businesses and quality brands. As a result, a fifth "P"—Participation—has taken its rightful place alongside Product, Price, Place, and Promotion in the traditional marketing mix, turning the top-down marketing funnel into a viral loop that benefits from word of mouth.

Facebook expands the reach of word of mouth and increases the speed at which it spreads. As a result, it has quickly become the platform of choice for businesses and their customers to connect and engage online. Regardless of whether your business or organization has a presence on Facebook, chances are that your customers/members do, so you should be there, too.

FRIEND-LY ADVICE

At the end of the day, marketing on Facebook is still marketing, so don't abandon everything you already know about marketing. You simply need to know how to apply your marketing savvy and expertise to Facebook.

Tapping the Power of Facebook's Promotional Features

Most users know that businesses and organizations can advertise on Facebook. Glance at the right side of nearly any Facebook page and you'll see at least one ad. What many businesses and organizations fail to realize, however, is that several of Facebook's promotional features are free. In the following sections, we introduce you to both the free and paid offerings and reveal how you can use them alone or together to rev up your promotional efforts on Facebook.

Launching a Facebook Page

Every business needs a home, and on Facebook the home of choice for a business, brand, celebrity, or organization is its Facebook page. Pages are meant for businesses and organizations to share news, opinions, and information about their products and services with Facebook members, or in the case of bands, celebrities, and authors, information about upcoming public appearances or the like. Packed with features that enable your business or organization to engage with fans (members who choose to Like your page), Facebook pages enable you to build relationships, which have the potential to lead to positive word-of-mouth advertising and brand evangelism.

By posting timely and clever status updates, which show up in members' News Feeds, page owners on Facebook find they're able to keep customers, prospects, and fans well informed of news, events, contests, special offers, and more, as well as drive traffic back to their websites.

Before Facebook, if you wanted to reach out to customers or stakeholders to inform them of, say, a contest, you relied on email or newsletters, which many people tend to ignore or overlook. With a Facebook page, a business or organization can post a status update announcing a promotion, and chances are fairly good that a fan will Like the update or even leave a comment, which can spark a chain reaction. The comment gets published in the fan's News Feed for all his friends to see and inspires other Facebook members to respond with their own comments, which in turn further promotes the promotion.

If you're a business owner or marketing manager focused on your return on investment (ROI) from engaging with customers and others (which we like to refer to as ROE—return on engagement), you'll be glad to know that Facebook pages come complete with a suite of free tools that enable you to measure how many fans interact with your page, how old they are, where they live, and more.

In short, if you have something to promote, build a page. We show you how in Chapter 16.

Posting Ads on Facebook

If all this "engagement" stuff has got you scratching your head and wondering whether you can just post an ad on Facebook promoting your products or services, then Facebook ads are for you. With 900,000,000+ active users, all of whom have supplied Facebook with their geographic and demographic information, Facebook ads enable you to reach only the people you want to target.

Suppose you're a wedding photographer and you want to target your ad exclusively toward women between the ages of 24 and 30 in a certain locale whose relationship status is Engaged. Well, on Facebook, you can. Similarly, if you own the hip new sushi restaurant in town, you can target your ads toward a specific demographic, and if you run a Colorado-based not-for-profit that takes high school kids on backcountry trips, you can target local or national wilderness enthusiasts to make a donation to your cause.

To learn more about Facebook ads, check out Chapter 18.

Going Viral with Facebook for Websites

Through status updates, notes, photos, videos, and more, your business can create quite an impressive presence on Facebook. But what if you're BlackPast.org, the Google of African American History, with 10,000 pages of content crying out to be shared with Facebook fans?

Copying and pasting all that content into individual notes or attempting to create a status update calling attention to each one of your web pages would be a nightmare, even for an intern! The solution to your problem (actually, more opportunity than problem) may be found in Facebook for Websites.

Think of Facebook for Websites as a set of programming tools that enables your website programmer to add certain Facebook features—like Share, Comment, Recent Friend Activity, and more—to your website. So in the preceding example, BlackPast.org can add Facebook's Share button to each of its 10,000 or so pages, which encourages its visitors to recommend the content to all their Facebook friends.

There's a lot more you can do with Facebook for Websites. To see for yourself, visit developers.facebook.com and click **Build for Websites**.

FRIEND-LY ADVICE

Implementing Facebook for Websites on your website isn't for amateur website builders. In many cases, it requires tapping in to Facebook's API (application programming interface), which is best left to skilled and creative website developers, engineers, and programmers.

Tapping the Power of Check-In Deals and Offers

And don't forget about using Facebook Offers and Facebook Check-in Deals to connect with customers when they're out and about. Facebook Offers enables you to create a special offer that members can claim and redeem at your physical location using their smartphone or other mobile device. You can also create Check-in Deals and run them across multiple store locations.

For more about using Facebook Offers and Check-in Deals in your business, check out Chapter 16.

Establishing a Following with Groups

Another option that businesses, brands, and organizations have for connecting and engaging with Facebook members is to create a Facebook group. Although groups have a similar look and feel to pages, Facebook intends for them to serve different purposes. While pages are managed by businesses or brands, groups tend to be managed by Facebook members and are great for connecting with high school classmates, organizing family members for a reunion or Mom's surprise seventy-fifth birthday party, generating discussion among book club members, and so on.

Although individuals—rather than businesses—tend to start and manage Facebook groups, that doesn't mean you can't use them for business purposes. Because you can set groups as private/ for members only, creating a group and inviting select business customers and brand advocates to join and engage with one another is a great way to facilitate focus groups and gain valuable insight into customer wants and needs.

Similarly, you can join groups that focus on topics related to your business, brand, or organization—assuming they're open to all Facebook members—and listen in to what people are saying. If appropriate to the situation, you can even respond officially as a company or organization representative.

For more information on Facebook groups, check out Chapter 9, where we show you how to join a group, form groups of your own, engage in group discussions, and share stuff with fellow group members.

Engaging Members with Facebook Applications (Apps)

Suppose you want your customers to be able to use your company website to share video testimonials about your business, photos of themselves using your products or services, or daily updates of their related activities. You'd spend a fortune designing, programming, and engineering your site to handle the activity and resulting traffic. Facebook handles all of that for you, and it doesn't cost you a cent.

Facebook's core applications—which include status updates, photos, and video—are all available for you to use for business purposes. Want to hold a promotion to see who can create the best video featuring your products or services? With Facebook's video application, your customers can upload user-generated video files to Facebook and post them to your page's Timeline, and you can call attention to them through status updates and notes.

With a little creativity, you're sure to figure out how your business can leverage Facebook's applications for business purposes. Let's say you run a chain of florist shops and you want your customers on Facebook to be able to send their Facebook friends virtual flower arrangements. As members send virtual flowers back and forth on Facebook, you gain valuable visibility among people most inclined to send real flowers later on.

Great idea! But because Facebook doesn't have a suitable application of its own, you'd have to build a virtual flower application in line with Facebook's standards and guidelines for applications. Sound complicated? It is, which is why you should work with a professional Facebook application developer—someone who has successfully built Facebook apps before and knows her way around Facebook's development landscape.

For a list of developers who can help your business build the Facebook application of your dreams, visit developers.facebook.com/ preferredmarketingdevelopers. There you find a list of experienced and trusted developers who are included in Facebook's Preferred Marketing Developer Program.

Do's and Don'ts of Doing Business on Facebook

If you're not careful, social-media marketing, particularly on Facebook, can do more harm than good. Attempting to go viral goes both ways: say the right thing, and the good word can spread like wildfire; say the wrong thing, and you'll be engulfed by that wildfire. To improve your odds of success, adhere to the following do's and don'ts of marketing on Facebook:

- **Do engage with your fans.** When a fan leaves a comment on one of your status updates, thank her, answer her question, or comment back (if appropriate). If a fan posts a photo or video on your Timeline, make a comment or click the **Like** button if, indeed, you appreciate the post.

- **Do be authentic and transparent.** We live in the age of reality, where everyone feels they're entitled to know everyone else's business. (You can thank reality TV and cable news for that.) On Facebook, the same holds true for your business. If you launch a Facebook page, fans expect you to be real, and that means transparent and authentic. No hidden agendas allowed.

- **Don't self-promote too much.** Remember, it's called social networking, not social selling. While your customers expect you to be on Facebook, they don't want you constantly accosting them with sales pitches.

- **Don't use "I" statements in status updates or notes.** A business is not an "I," it's a "We." If you post a status update about exhibiting at a conference or trade show, you wouldn't say, "I am exhibiting at such-and-such show later this week. Stop by and see me in booth number 513." Rather, you'd write something like, "XYZ Products will be exhibiting at such-and-such show later this week. Stop by and see us in booth number 513."

- **Do flesh out your Profile.** Be complete, and include everything you're asked to provide in your Profile. Don't leave your fans—your customers and prospects—hanging. Give them all the information they need.

- **Don't create multiple pages for multiple products.** You may not have the resources to keep all the pages up to date and relevant, not to mention that you'll dilute your brand.

- **Do create and post notes.** Like entries on company blogs, Facebook Notes have the potential to be indexed by search engines, which means your notes—if packed with great keywords and phrases, and relevant to your customers and branding goals—can help attract more fans and traffic.

- **Don't go long stretches without posting a status update.** Fans and passersby have a reasonable expectation that your Facebook page is going to be kept up to date, and the number-one way of doing that is to create and post a constant stream of status updates. One to two updates per day is ideal, but if you can't do that, twice a week should suffice.

- **Don't put all your engagement eggs in one basket.** Facebook is not the be-all, end-all marketing vehicle. It's just one more weapon in what should be a multi-channel marketing arsenal.

- **Don't forget everything you already know about marketing.** Facebook is just like every other marketing channel—you have to know your audience and what's considered the most acceptable way to engage with that audience in that particular channel.

- **Do measure your efforts.** ROI on Facebook comes by way of ROE (return on engagement). Areas to measure include the reach of your status updates, website traffic from Facebook, search engine results and ranking, inbound links to your website, number of fans or group members, comments on status updates, mentions of your brand as a result of your Facebook-related activity, and more.

The Least You Need to Know

- The business case for Facebook? 900,000,000+ people happily gathered in one central location online, many of whom are your customers and expect to see your business or brand there.

- At the very least, your business or organization should have its own page to function as its base of operations on Facebook.

- Cross-promote your Facebook page and company website to drive traffic to each.

- Facebook ads give you the power to target Facebook users by locale and demographic.

- Use the Groups feature and business apps to further engage customers and prospects on Facebook.

Launching and Managing a Facebook Page

In This Chapter

- Grasping Facebook page basics
- Building and customizing a page
- Keeping your page fresh with relevant, compelling content
- Attracting traffic
- Tracking results with Page Insights (analytics)

Facebook offers pages as a way for businesses, brands, organizations, and celebrities to establish a presence online and connect with customers, fans, and others using the world's most popular social network. A page enables you to share your business or organization and any products or services you offer with Facebook members.

A Facebook page can function as a central location for your business or organization on Facebook, or you can use a page to highlight very specific products or services. Through your pages, you can post status updates, as well as pictures and videos, to keep current and prospective customers informed and up to date.

Build a quality page, populate it with relevant and compelling content, and you're likely to attract fans. When fans interact with your page, these interactions can appear in their News Feeds, where their friends can find out about your page and business and help spread the word. Do it right, and you might be able to spark a word-of-mouth promotional wildfire that advertises for you! In this chapter, we show you how.

POKE

Organizations, products, or services that have a strong brand presence often find that they're already on Facebook. Facebook members may create their own Facebook groups or pages where they discuss an organization's merits (or shortcomings) or review its products or services. This can be very positive for your organization, but you should still launch an official page of your own so you can play a leadership role in any associated communities. You can then invite members of the other communities, who have already expressed an interest in your offerings, to become fans of your page by Liking it.

Crafting and Customizing Your Page

Your page is your business's or organization's face on Facebook, so you want it to create a good and lasting first impression. You want people who see it to Like it and become fans so you can communicate with them directly. In the following sections, we show you how to lay the groundwork for a quality page and then step you through the process of creating it.

POKE

To create a page, you need to be the official representative of a business, organization, or other entity, such as a rock band; a celebrity; or a business unto yourself, such as Kate Milhouse Dentistry. After creating the page, you can add other page administrators (admins) to help post content and monitor activity. If you're not officially authorized to create a page for a business or organization, then create a group instead, as explained in Chapter 9.

Laying the Groundwork

Just because Facebook pages are free to create doesn't mean they should look cheap. Invest at least as much time preparing to create a page as you would spend on creating a quality advertisement for your organization. Prior to creating a page, make sure the following pieces are in place:

- **Purpose:** Generally speaking, the first goal of your page should be to convince visitors to become fans by clicking the **Like** button and regularly engaging with your business or organization on Facebook. You might also have a secondary goal, such as encouraging Facebook members to visit your organization's website, keep fans in the loop concerning newsworthy events, gather insight into customer wants and needs, or inform fans of special deals and offers on your products and services. Your ultimate goal might be to sell, but when it comes to Facebook, selling shouldn't be the purpose; instead, you should use your page to warm up prospects and customers, create community, and build trust.

- **Page name:** Settle on a name for your page that clearly and specifically identifies your business and organization and what you do or sell. Facebook prohibits the use of generic names of products and services, such as "Pizza" or "Wedding Photography," so use names more like "Brighton Feed & Saddlery" or "Homemade harvey." Pick a name that sets you apart and is recognizable and easy to remember.

- **Quality images:** You'll need two high-quality images to start: one large, captivating cover image that represents your business or organization and a smaller image (Facebook recommends using a logo) that represents your business or organization as a thumbnail image as you share content, and interact with fans and other pages on Facebook, and post ads (if you choose to do so).

- **Content:** Content is key in turning fans into customers and customers into fans via Facebook. Focus your efforts on serving the community rather than your own interests. Posting your entire product catalog is probably a bad idea, because it sends a clear message that you're only interested in selling products and collecting money. Instead, consider posting a tip on how customers can enhance their experience with a particular product.

> **POKE**
>
> Remember, it's called *social networking,* not *social selling.* Although the majority of Facebook members expect businesses and organizations to have a presence on Facebook and other social-networking platforms and services, a much smaller percentage want to be marketed to. Post compelling content, and your fans will evangelize for you.

Creating Your Page

The process of creating a page is relatively easy. You click a link, enter your preferences and content via a series of forms, and your page is up and running. The following list leads you through the process step by step:

1. Scroll to the bottom of the Facebook screen you're on (down to the footer) and click **Create a Page**. Six options appear.

2. Do one of the following depending on the type of page you're creating:

   - Click **Local Business or Place**, select the category that best describes your business, and fill in the requested information.

   - Click **Company, Organization, or Institution** and then select the category that most closely represents the company, organization, or institution you want to promote.

   - Click **Brand or Product** and then select the category that most closely represents the brand or product you're going to promote.

   - Click **Artist, Band, or Public Figure** and select the category for the artist, band, or public figure you want to promote.

   - Click **Entertainment** and choose the category of the entity you want to promote.

   - Click **Cause or Community** and type in the name of the cause or community you want to promote.

3. Click the check box next to "I agree to Facebook Pages Terms."

4. Click **Get Started**. Facebook displays a setup screen prompting you to upload a Profile picture for your page.

5. Follow the on-screen guide to upload a Profile picture for your page and perform any other steps you're instructed to perform to create your page. (Steps vary depending on the type of page, and you might be able to skip some steps.)

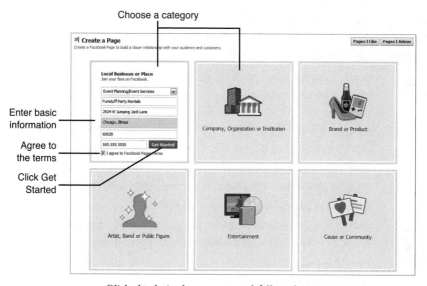

Click the desired page type and follow the on-screen instructions.

When you're done, Facebook displays your new page and highlights the Like button. Be sure to click the **Like** button, so when people visit your page, they see that at least one person likes it. Liking the page also helps promote it by including the fact that you Liked the page as part of your recent activities. After you click the Like button, Facebook leads you through some other basic page promotional and setup tasks, including inviting your friends to Like your page and share something on the page, so it's more than just a blank page.

Touring the Admin Panel

When you're done roughing out your page, Facebook displays it along with an Admin Panel at the top, which others won't see when they visit your page. Click **Hide** to hide the Admin Panel at any time, and click **Admin Panel** (upper-right corner) to bring it back into view.

The Admin Panel features numerous tools for managing your page and monitoring activity on your page. At the time we were writing this book, the Admin Panel featured the following:

- **Manage button/menu:** The Manage button provides options for editing your page (see "Editing Your Page," later in this chapter), displaying your Page's Activity Log (an unfiltered version of the Timeline), managing a list of banned users, protecting your page, and choosing to use your page identity instead of your personal identity to post content to the page. The Protect Your Page option enables you to verify that you're the official representative of the business or organization, so someone else can't claim the page or get administrative rights without your permission.

- **Build Audience button/menu:** This button opens a menu that offers several options for promoting your page. See "Building and Maintaining Your Fan Base" for additional details about promoting your page on and off Facebook.

- **Help button/menu:** Facebook provides gobs of help for creating, maintaining, and promoting pages. Options on the Help button/menu enable you to visit the Help Center, take a tour of the page's feature, view the Pages Product Guide, watch the Learning Video, and send feedback about the pages feature to Facebook.

- **Hide button:** Click the **Hide** button to hide the Admin Panel. When you hide the Panel, the Admin Panel button appears, which you can click to bring the Panel back into view.

- **Notifications:** This area provides a list of recent activities related to your page that you might want to know, such as the fact that someone on Facebook posted an update or commented on something you posted.

- **Messages:** By default, Facebook displays a Message button on your page that users can click to send your business, organization, or brand a private message instead of posting to your page's Timeline. (You can hide the Message button by editing your page, as explained later in this chapter. Look on the Manage Permissions tab of the page editing options.)

- **New Likes:** If a Facebook member Likes the page, that Like is listed here.

- **Insights:** If at least 30 Facebook members like your page, Facebook displays statistics about your page activity, so you can measure the success of your page and make educated decisions on how to more effectively achieve your goals.

- **Page Tips:** Check out Page Tips for suggestions on how to make your page more engaging, promote your page, and make better use of its many features. Click **Next** to view the next tip.

Click Hide if you want to hide the Admin Panel

Your page appears along with the Admin Panel.

Getting Back to Your Page

After creating your page, you can always return to the administrative area to make changes. Regardless of what you're doing in Facebook, click **Home** (in the top menu), and then click the name of the page (in the left menu). The selected page appears as a visitor will see it. You can click **Admin Panel** (upper-right corner) to display options for managing your page.

Editing Your Page

You can edit your page at any time to change the information you entered, change permissions, add or remove administrators, and more. We recommend that you at least check out the various edit options immediately after creating your page, so you know what's available. To edit your Page, display the Admin Panel, click the **Manage** button (near the top), and click **Edit Page**. (You can always return to the page at any time by clicking the **View Page** button in the upper-right corner.)

To edit any of the settings or access any of the administrative areas of the page, click the appropriate link in the left menu. You can adjust the following items:

- **Your Settings:** Here, you can set preferences for how your posts to your page appear and whether you'd like to receive email notifications when people post or comment on your page. We recommend keeping the default setting for both items. When posting to your page, you should always do so as the page because there's no "I" when communicating on behalf of a business or brand. Leaving **Posting Preferences** checked ensures all your posts will be displayed as coming from the same name associated with the page, not the name associated with your personal Facebook account. **Email Notifications** are important because they keep you informed whenever someone posts to your page.

- **Manage Permissions:** These options enable you to limit access to your page to only the countries you specify, set a minimum age for accessing the page, or change the page's visibility status. We recommend changing Page Visibility to "Unpublish page" until your page is ready for prime time. Other options here enable you to control who can post to the page's Timeline, prohibit the posting of photos or videos, restrict post visibility and tagging, display or hide the Messages button, and filter undesirable content. Manage Permissions is also where you go if you want to delete the page.

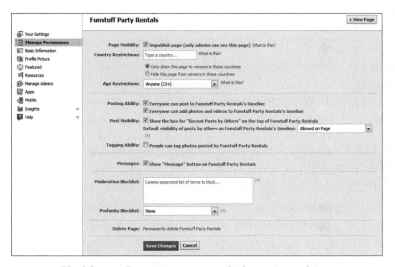

Use Manage Permissions to control who can post what to your page.

- **Basic Information:** Here you're able to add and edit basic information about your business, organization, brand, or cause, including the startup date, hours of operation, email address and phone number, website address, and so on.
- **Profile Picture:** This is where you add, edit, or remove your Profile picture. You can either browse for an image on your computer to upload or take a picture of yourself if you're personally the subject of the page. You can even edit your thumbnail image.

- **Featured:** These settings pertain to featuring other pages and your own page's admins on the page. When you use Facebook As Page (as opposed to using your personal Facebook account to interact with your page), your page has the opportunity to Like other pages. Once your page Likes another page, the Liked page is displayed on the left side of your page. The **Add Featured Likes** setting enables you to identify which of the pages your page Likes are featured on your page. The **Add Featured Page Owners** setting enables you to publicly display your page's admins on your page.

- **Resources:** Here you find links to areas of Facebook that are helpful for making your page more engaging and promoting your page by advertising it on Facebook, inviting email contacts, using social plugins, and linking the page to your Twitter account, if you have one.

- **Manage Admins:** Here you control who, besides you, can administer the page. Because most businesses and organizations have more than one person capable of managing their page, Facebook enables you to assign an unlimited number of admins. Admins, who access your page through their personal accounts, by default remain anonymous to your page's users and can have their privileges revoked at any time by the page's creator.

- **Apps:** As we discuss in Chapter 12, your Facebook account comes preloaded with apps, and the same is true for a Facebook page. Here, you can adjust settings for Photos, Events, Notes, Videos, and any other apps you add, or you can delete individual apps altogether. For example, you can click **Edit Settings** below Events to add an Events tab to your page and enable or disable the capability for Events to publish content to your page.

- **Mobile:** Mobile enables you to sign up to receive text messages from Facebook notifying you of activity on your page. See Chapter 14 for more about Facebook Mobile.

- **Insights:** If you want to learn about the people who Like your page and how they interact with your content, click **Insights**. Once 30 people Like your page, you'll find all sorts of stats and data here, including the number of active users broken down by day, week, and month; number of post views and items commented on; user demographics, including age, gender, and geographical location; and more.

- **Help:** Clicking **Help** takes you to the Facebook pages help area, where you can find out more about creating, managing, and promoting pages and find links for posting a question to the Pages forum, reporting bugs, and submitting suggestions to Facebook.

- **Deals:** Click **Deals** to reward customers for checking in to your page, as explained later in this chapter in the section "Rewarding Customers with Check-In Deals."

POKE

Facebook allows you to assign one of five "roles"—manager, content creator, moderator, advertiser, and insights analyst—to your page's admins. The manager role maintains all permissions and can do everything allowed on the page. The creator role can do everything but manage admin roles. The moderator role can respond to and delete comments, send messages as the page, create ads, and view Insights. The advertiser role is limited to creating ads and viewing insights, while the insights analyst does just that. To assign roles, visit the page you manage, click **edit page** above the Admin Panel, and click **Admin Roles** in the left column.

Rearranging Apps and Views

Just below your cover image are thumbnails for apps and views. You and whoever visits your page can click these thumbnails to focus on specific content, such as photos, Likes, and map entries. The Photos thumbnail is a permanent fixture; you can't remove it or move it. You can't remove the Likes or Maps thumbnails, either, but you can move them and you can move or remove thumbnails for any apps you use:

- To move a thumbnail, click the arrow on the right side of the thumbnail area to expand it, mouse over a thumbnail you want to move, click the edit button in the upper-right corner of the thumbnail, and choose the option to **Swap position with** the thumbnail of choice.

- To remove a thumbnail you've added, click the arrow on the right side of the thumbnail area to expand it, mouse over a thumbnail you want to move, click the edit button in the upper-right corner of the thumbnail, and click **Remove from Favorites**.

Adding Compelling Content to Your Page

Your business, brand, or organization page is very similar to your personal Timeline, complete with an option to add a cover image, an About link for fleshing out your business's or organization's profile, thumbnails for Photos and other apps, and a Timeline you can post to. Use your page just as you use your personal Timeline to engage fans, keep them coming back for more, and inspire them to share your page with their friends. (See Chapter 3 for details about navigating and posting to the Timeline.)

Page Timelines differ somewhat from personal Timelines. With your page Timeline, you have the following options:

- **Pin a weekly post:** After you post a status update, photo, video, event, or milestone, you can pin it for up to seven days to the top of the Timeline. Mouse over the post, click the edit button in the upper-right corner, and click **Pin to Top**.

- **Star a post:** Mouse over a post and click the star icon in the upper-right corner to expand the post to the full width of the Timeline. You can change the post back to normal size at any time by clicking the star icon again.

- **Post a milestone:** If you're rolling out a new product, launching a fundraising event, opening a new store, attending a conference, or engaging in some other significant activity (either past or present), consider posting it as a milestone. Click **Event, Milestone +** at the top of the Publisher, followed by **Event, Milestone**, or **Question**, and follow the on-screen guidance to complete your post. Milestones expand to the full width of the Timeline to increase their visibility.

- **Change post dates:** You can pre-date items you post, so you can post about milestones and events that have already occurred. When posting a milestone or event, Facebook prompts you to choose a date. If you already posted the milestone or event, hover over it, click the edit button in the upper-right corner, change the date, and click **Save**.

When posting content to your business, brand, or organization page's Timeline, *engage* is the keyword. Your page isn't as much about you, your business, or your products as it is about the topics your fans are interested in. We're not saying you should pander to the masses; that could turn fans off, too. You want to size up your audience and deliver the content they crave in a way that meets or exceeds their expectations. If you're in the restaurant biz, that may mean posting this week's specials. If you're promoting your band, it might mean posting lyrics to your most popular song or updates about the current tour. If you manufacture 120 different styles of motorcycle seats, you may end up fielding lots of customer-service questions about motorcycle seat fitment. Treat your fans like friends instead of customers or clients, and you're likely to hit the bull's-eye.

Facebook has a vested interest in the success of your page, because it has the potential of drawing more users to Facebook, so it offers suggestions on how to make your page engaging. To access these suggestions, click the **Manage** button in your page's Admin Panel, click **Edit Page**, click **Resources**, and click the **Best practices guides to make your Page engaging**.

Use your page to engage fans the same way you use your personal Timeline to engage friends.

WHOA!

Resist the urge to post your product catalog. Far too many businesses treat social media, which is intended to be dynamic and interactive, as a shell for static web content. They essentially copy web content and post it on Facebook. This is ineffective and likely to do more harm than good.

Rewarding Customers with Check-In Deals

Facebook's Check-in Deals enable you to reward loyalty while enlisting your loyal customers to promote your business. When a user visits your business, she can "check in" on Facebook and then redeem the Deal, for example, by presenting it as displayed on her smartphone. (When we were writing this, Facebook charged businesses nothing to offer Check-in Deals.)

To create a Check-in Deal, head to your page, display the Admin Panel, click **Manage**, click **Edit Page**, and click **Deals** (in the left column). The Create a Deal page appears, prompting you to specific details, including the type of Deal, restrictions, instructions on how to claim the Deal, and maximum redemptions.

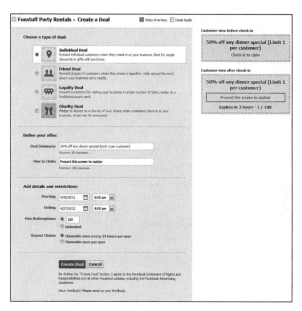

*Create a Facebook Deal to reward customers for checking
in to your page on Facebook.*

Offering an Offer

At the time of this writing, Facebook began beta testing a new ad format called Offers. Initially available to a small number of businesses in the United States, New Zealand, Singapore, Australia, Japan, and Turkey, Offers is expected to be available to most businesses on Facebook by the time you get to this point in the book.

Facebook Offers enables businesses and organizations to present specials and coupons to fans via posts that appear in users' News Feeds on both the desktop and mobile versions of Facebook. Once an Offer is claimed, the user simply displays it on his mobile device's screen or prints and brings a copy of the Offer to the merchant's location to redeem it.

If your business operates out of a physical store location, or you're setting up a booth at a trade show or conference where a high volume of traffic will be nearby, consider creating a Facebook Offer. And because claiming these Offers results in a social action—news about it is automatically shared with the member's friends on Facebook—a well-crafted Offer should bring rave reviews to you and your business.

To create an Offer, click **Offer, Event +** in the Publisher, followed by **Offer** (at the top of resulting list). You'll notice that the Publisher changes appearance and prompts you to **Upload Thumbnail**, **Write a headline for your offer** (up to 90 characters is allowed), set the number of claims you'll accept, determine an expiration date, and **Add your terms and conditions**.

Creating a Facebook Offer to find new customers and engage with more of your fans.

Expanding Content with Other Facebook Apps

In addition to posting status updates and photos, facilitating discussions, and offering Check-in Deals, consider using other Facebook applications to engage the people who Like your page. You can use the Events app to announce special occasions, such as a grand opening, a conference, or a trade show. You can post a note to focus the spotlight on your "Fan of the Month," announce the results of a recent promotion, or ask fans to share tips for getting more out of a featured product. Use your imagination to think up clever ways to use Facebook's standard apps to boost engagement.

Accessorizing Your Page with Third-Party Apps

To further enhance your page, you can add business apps from third-party developers. Following are some examples:

- **Promotions** for pages enable you to run branded, interactive promotions on your pages, including sweepstakes, contests, coupon giveaways, instant wins, gifting, and quizzes.

- **Testimonials** and **Reviews** enable you to collect customer testimonials and product/service reviews from Facebook fans and display them on your page.

- **Eventbrite** provides tools for bringing people together for an event and selling tickets. If you're a budding rock star, this app could come in very handy.

- **Polls** make it easy to create online polls and analyze results with graphs that illustrate user responses across multiple demographics.

The procedure for adding third-party apps to your page varies depending on the app. To find out more about a business app and how to add it to your page, use the Search box at the top of any Facebook page to track down the app's page. For some apps, the page might include an Add to Page link, typically located in the lower-left corner of the page. (For general information about apps, including how to find apps on Facebook, see Chapter 12.)

Building and Maintaining Your Fan Base

"If you build it, they will come," is as untrue a statement on Facebook as it is throughout the rest of the web. Building, growing, and maintaining an active community of fans through a Facebook page requires the following two key components:

- **A killer page** with fresh, engaging, and interactive content.

- **Promotion.** Yep, that's right. You build a page to promote something, and then you have to promote your page. It never stops.

Facebook can't help you with the first component. It's entirely up to you to keep the content on your page fresh and compelling and interact with fans regularly and in a meaningful way. Facebook does, however, provide you with several tools for promoting your page:

- **Become your own number-one fan.** Pull up your page and click the **Like** button (to the right of the page title). Now at least your page has one fan. When you become a fan, all your friends are notified via their News Feeds.

- **Invite Facebook friends and email contacts.** Display the Admin panel, click the **Build Audience** button (near the top), click **Invite Email Contacts** or **Invite Friends**, and follow the on-screen instructions to complete the operation. Facebook distributes your invitations for you.

- **Share your page on your personal Timeline.** Display the Admin Panel, click the **Build Audience button** (near the top), click **Share Page**, and use the resulting dialog box to share your page as a link on your personal Timeline. When you share a link on your Timeline, it's likely to appear in your friends' News Feeds, and hopefully, they'll share it with their Friends.

- **Link your page to Twitter.** Twitter is a very popular microblogging platform. If you don't have a Twitter account yet, register for one at twitter.com and then edit your page to link it to Twitter. In the Admin Panel, click the **Manage** button, click **Edit Page**, click **Resources** (on the left), click **Link your Page to Twitter**, click **Link a Page to Twitter** (*not* Link My Profile to Twitter), and follow the on-screen instructions.

- **Promote your Facebook page on your website or blog.** Use Facebook badges, Like buttons, and other tools to link back to your Facebook page. See Chapter 17 for details on how to cross-promote your Facebook page and other online properties.

POKE

Facebook is very particular about the way you promote your page. Click the **Best Practice for Marketing on Facebook** link inside the **Resources** area of your page's settings for additional guidance on promoting your Facebook page outside Facebook.

Tracking Page Effectiveness with Page Insights

Wondering how many people visit your page every day? Want to know the number and demographics of your Facebook fans and how frequently fans interact with your page? Then pull up your Page Insights (Facebook's term for analytics). From your page's Admin Panel, next to the Insights box, click **See All**. Here you'll find vital metrics related to your page's performance, including daily, weekly, and monthly active users; unique page views; gender and age of your visitors; countries, cities, and languages of your visitors; and more.

To get the most out of your business activities on Facebook, you need to know what's working and what's not, which content your fans interact with most, and how fans interact with your brand and with one another. While you can glean some of this information from scanning each individual item on your page's Wall, doing so is tedious and prone to miscalculation.

Enter Page Insights. From posting quality scores that measure how engaging your posts have been over a rolling seven-day period, to the number of fans interacting with your content and the number of interactions per post, Facebook provides the information you need to quickly evaluate the effectiveness of your efforts and your return on investment (ROI).

Facebook also emails you a weekly summary of your Insights, informing you of the number of fans you've gained (or lost) during the week; the number of Timeline posts, comments, and Likes; and the number of visits to the page. The message includes links to various Facebook features that can help you build your user base.

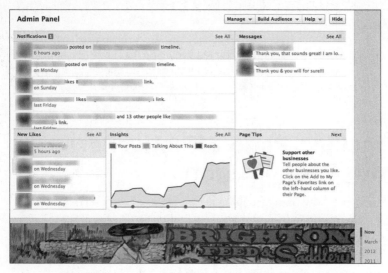

Page Insights present valuable statistics related to your page.

The Least You Need to Know

- To create a page, log in to Facebook, scroll to the bottom, click **Create a Page**, and follow the on-screen instructions.

- When you leave your page and need to return to it, click **Home** and click the name of your page in the left column.

- Your page contains a Hide button in the upper-right corner. Click **Hide** to hide the Admin Panel, and click the **Admin Panel** button to get it back.

- After creating your page, display the Admin Panel and click the **Help** button for links to all the help you need for creating, maintaining, and promoting an engaging page that will help you achieve your Facebook promotional goals.

- This is social networking. It's not social selling. Use your page to interact with customers and brand advocates as you would interact with colleagues and Facebook friends.

- Use Page Insights to measure and monitor traffic, evaluate ROI, and identify obstacles to engagement.

Cross-Promoting Facebook

In This Chapter

- Recognizing the importance and power of cross-promoting your online properties
- Implementing a few basic cross-promotional strategies
- Linking your website or blog to Facebook using social plugins
- Helping Facebook members automatically spread your news as they access your site content

Which came first, Facebook or the internet? To hear some people talk about it, Facebook *is* the internet, but of course we know better than to go there. When Al Gore took the initiative in creating the internet (err, we mean, when Sir Timothy John Berners-Lee invented the mark-up language that would lead to the launch of the World Wide Web in 1989), Mark Zuckerberg—Facebook's founder—was just six years old and probably couldn't type. Some 22 or so years later, and some businesses still think all they need is a Facebook business or brand page and all their business-related goals will magically come true.

Not true, and in the following sections we tell you why your website is just as important—if not more so—than your presence on Facebook, and how to make both entities work in blissful harmony.

If You Build It, Will They Come?

Facebook presents the classic "If you build it, will they come" conundrum. On the one hand, your customers or brand advocates might think to search for you on Facebook, and if they do happen to find your page, they're likely to become fans. On the other hand, although the majority of Facebook members expect your business or organization to have a presence on Facebook, they rarely, if ever, search for you. Rather, they affiliate because of something you've done to inform them of your presence on Facebook, like posting a "Find us on Facebook" badge on your website or blog or sending a special email message to them promoting your page.

At the end of the day, you have more control over your own website than you'll ever have over Facebook. From the domain name, visual look and feel, and the underlying code, to the site's navigation, copy, and capability to scale according to your business needs and priorities, a website has the potential to be infinitely more valuable to your business or organization than your page on Facebook.

Still, it does seem to some that if your business is not on Facebook, well, you're just not on the internet. For this reason and many others, it is just to leverage your website in ways that drive traffic to and from Facebook.

Cross-Promoting the Simple Way

Cross-promotion is crucial to building a fan base on Facebook. Take every opportunity to let your customers know about your Facebook page and why they should want to become fans. If you run a retail storefront, restaurant, or office, print some postcards or small business/information cards promoting your Facebook address, and make sure everyone receives one on his way out the door.

Add Facebook's "f" logo to your company e-newsletter, all of your email marketing communications, and, of course, your website and blog. Heck, you might even go so far as to print your Facebook address on the company letterhead! If it works, go for it. At the very least, do the simple things to build a following on Facebook.

> **FRIEND-LY ADVICE**
>
> Facebook is particular about how and where exactly you use its logo. For usage guidelines and approved versions of the "f" logo, visit facebook.com/brandpermissions/logos.php.

Another simple way of promoting is to link your Facebook account to Twitter—the popular microblogging platform. If your business doesn't have a Twitter account, register for one at twitter.com and then edit your Facebook page to link it to Twitter. This option is available by visiting www.facebook.com/twitter.

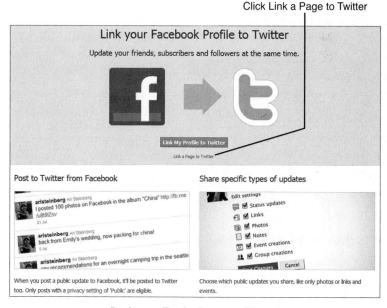

Link your Facebook page to Twitter.

Using Social Plugins on Your Website

Facebook created social plugins so people visiting your website can have a personalized and social experience that's familiar to them and that helps your content and site gain greater visibility. When your website visitors interact with social plugins from Facebook, they're able to share their experiences and observations about your site and its content with their friends and others on Facebook.

Facebook's primary social plugins include these:

- **Like or Share button.** Facebook's Like or Share button lets the people who visit your website or blog share pages from your site back to Facebook with a single click. When people click the Like or Share button on a page, they're not only letting you know that they like what you posted, but they're actually recommending your content to their friends.

- **Send button.** If you think it'd be a good idea for your website or blog visitors to be able to send what they see on your site to anyone with an email address or Facebook account, then the Send button is for you.

- **Comments box.** One of the primary characteristics of a blog is the capability for visitors to leave and read comments on a post-by-post basis. With Facebook's Comments box installed on your website or blog, when someone who's logged on to Facebook posts a comment on your site, that comment is shared on Facebook, too. As a result, more people see the engagement taking place on your website.

- **Activity feed.** With Facebook's Activity Feed installed on your website or blog, visitors are able to see what their Facebook friends are commenting on, Liking, or sharing right on your site.

- **Like box.** Not to be confused with the Like button, Facebook's Like box lets visitors to your website or blog Like your Facebook page and view its most recent stream of activity directly from your site, including who Likes your page and your latest status updates.

- **Registration.** Facebook's Registration plugin enables your website users, if they're required to sign in to your site, to do so using a Facebook username and password. When visitors are already logged into Facebook, the login form on your website is already populated with everything they need to log in to your site with the click of one button.

The Facebook Share button

Use social plugins to link your site to Facebook.

To gain access to the code necessary to make these and other "social plugins" work on your website or blog, click **Edit Page** (at the top of your page's Admin Panel), and then click **Update Info**, followed by **Resources** in the left column and the **Use social plugins** link (under Connect with people) on the next page.

POKE

Unless you're a skilled webmaster or really understand the code that lives underneath your website or blog, don't waste your time trying to place Facebook's social plugin code yourself. Save time and frustration by instead working with a skilled programmer, because although Facebook makes it easy to get around and install apps on Facebook. com, your website is an entirely different beast unto itself.

Sharing News Socially and Automatically

Recently, a number of online businesses and organizations, including Mashable, The Daily Show, MSNBC, and others, have developed "social news apps" that enable their website visitors to automatically share what they're reading and watching with their friends back on Facebook. When a Facebook member who's logged in to Facebook and has authorized the social news app does anything on the associated website, such as reading a particular article, that action is automatically broadcast through the member's News Feed and shared with his or her Facebook Friends.

Think about it. Wouldn't you like all of my 1,000 or so friends on Facebook to know I just visited your website or blog and read an article or blog post you published there? Of course you would. The possibility that your content could go viral without your doing anything special (aside, of course, from developing a well-conceived social news app and offering it via Facebook) is huge.

Although Facebook doesn't offer a turnkey social news app for you to install on your website or blog, it does provide resources and guidance for developers who want to pursue such opportunities. For more information, have your webmaster visit developers.facebook.com/docs/opengraph.

The Least You Need to Know

- Make sure people know where to find you on and off Facebook by linking your Facebook properties to your blogs and websites and vice versa.
- For usage guidelines and approved versions of the "f" logo, visit facebook.com/brandpermissions/logos.php, and then include the Facebook logo on all of your promotional materials.

- Visit www.facebook.com/twitter to find out how to link your Facebook and Twitter accounts.

- To access social plugins, create a page (as explained in Chapter 16), click **Manage** (at the top of your page's Admin Panel), **Edit Page**, **Resources**, and **Use social plugins** (under Connect with people).

- For information on how to create and use social news apps, have your webmaster visit developers.facebook.com/docs/opengraph.

Mastering the Soft Sell with Social Ads

In This Chapter

- Recognizing the potential of Facebook ads
- Using Facebook ads strategically in your marketing campaigns
- Doing the essential prep work
- Following Facebook's rules and regulations for posting ads
- Creating a Facebook ad that achieves your goals

Posting advertisements for your business or organization on Facebook via a personal status update is like announcing a 75-percent-off sale during the singing of "The Star-Spangled Banner." It'll earn you more enemies than friends. You can get away with it on a business page, as explained in Chapter 15, but don't do it from your personal Facebook account. If you want to advertise, you should carefully craft and post ads using Facebook Ads—the site's official advertising platform.

In this chapter, we introduce you to the potential benefits (and a few drawbacks) of Facebook advertising, step you through the process of developing an effective strategy, show you how to prepare your ads, and then assist you in launching and managing your advertising campaign.

Weighing the Pros and Cons of Facebook Ads

You can receive a great deal of word-of-mouth advertising on Facebook without spending a penny, so you may be wondering whether paid advertising is worth it. We can't answer that question for you, because each business's or organization's goals are different, but we can provide you with the pros and cons to consider in making this decision for yourself.

FRIEND-LY ADVICE

Doing business on Facebook is more about relationship marketing than intrusion marketing. Don't expect to see a big boost in sales when you first start posting ads on Facebook. Consider using ads to develop a greater presence and following on Facebook by encouraging Facebook members to become fans of your page, join your brand-based group, or register for a special event.

Potential Benefits

When deciding where to invest your advertising budget, consider the following benefits of Facebook ads:

- **More than 900 million active members:** A lot of people spend a lot of time on Facebook—even more time than they spend watching TV, glancing at billboards, reading newspapers or magazines, or browsing the web. In other words, they're more likely to see an ad on Facebook than anywhere else.

- **Ability to target a specific demographic and locale:** Facebook enables you to target your ads by age, gender, education, geography, marital status, and more, so you stand to get more bang for your buck than with more generalized CPC (cost-per-click) advertising on the web. In addition, Facebook members are more motivated to provide accurate information about themselves and keep it up to date, meaning your ads are more likely to be viewed by people who are who they say they are.

- **Ability to target keywords:** You can direct your ad to be displayed only to those members whose interests and activities align with keywords and phrases of your own choosing.

- **Potential bump from social interaction:** Your ad can include a call to action to do something on Facebook, such as become a fan or join a group. Whenever someone performs that call to action, it's likely to be posted to her Timeline and News Feed where her friends can see it. This provides extra mileage for your ad.

- **Affordability and scalability:** You can spend as much or as little money per day as you like on your Facebook ads. Facebook charges by cost per click (CPC) or cost per thousand impressions (CPM; the M stands for the "milli" in the metric system, not "millions"). *Impression* means that the ad appears on a member's screen when he's using Facebook, regardless of whether a user clicks it or even sees it.

- **Ability to measure your ad's performance:** Facebook provides detailed analytics so you can check your account for each ad's clicks, impressions, CPC, and CPM.

Potential Drawbacks

Facebook ads may seem like the ideal solution for businesses or organizations of any size, but they're not without some potential drawbacks, including the following:

- **Lack of interest in ads:** People on Facebook gather to connect and chat, not shop. Your ads are more like billboards or magazine advertisements that people may glance at in the midst of doing something else.

- **Poor timing versus search engine marketing:** When web users search using Google, Yahoo!, Bing, or other search engines, they're often trying to find an answer, solution, product, or service. With search-engine marketing, your ad catches them at the right time. This doesn't occur on Facebook, because Facebook is about connecting, not searching.

- **Lack of trust:** Facebook isn't very selective in determining who can advertise. As a result, many ads promote questionable products or services that turn off Facebook users to *all* ads.

Laying the Groundwork

You can slap together a Facebook ad in minutes, but before launching your first advertising campaign, spend some time brushing up on Facebook's rules and regulations, developing a strategy, and preparing the components of your ad—your message and graphic.

Brushing Up on Facebook Ads Rules and Regulations

To remain in good standing with Facebook, follow its rules. For an exhaustive (and exhausting) list of rules, head to facebook.com/ad_guidelines.php. The following list highlights the major do's and don'ts:

- No multiple accounts or automated creation of accounts for advertising purposes.
- No funny business on landing pages your ads link to, including pop-overs, pop-unders, fake close buttons, or bait-and-switch URLs (a link that makes visitors think they're going to a particular place but end up somewhere else).
- No using the Facebook name, brand, or logos in a way that even hints that Facebook endorses you, your company, or your products.
- No false, fraudulent, or deceptive ads.
- No lewd, crude, or otherwise inappropriate language or obscene, libelous, harassing, insulting, or unlawful content, including hate speech.

- No advertising weapons and explosives, illicit drugs and tobacco, scams, get-rich-quick schemes, adult "friend finders," uncertified pharmaceutical products, non-accredited colleges, or other goods or services that could be deemed dangerous, illegal, or of questionable value.

- Adhere to all of Facebook's privacy guidelines regarding member content.

- No spamming.

- Ads for alcoholic beverages or adult-related products or services must be age appropriate and not designed to lure minors; and ads for gambling-related services, including any online casinos, sports books, bingo, or poker, may not be posted without authorization from Facebook.

- No copyright infringement.

- No using ads to trick users into downloading spyware or malware.

Setting a Measurable Goal

To determine how well an advertising campaign is performing, start with a measurable goal. With a Facebook ad, you typically want to set two measurable goals: one relating to traffic and the other to conversion rates. Specify how much traffic or what percentage increase in traffic from Facebook to your Facebook page, non-Facebook landing page, or website you expect your ad campaign to generate. For conversion rates, specify the percentage of people who arrived from Facebook and then succeeded in performing the call to action included in the ad or on the resulting page or website.

The goals you set are entirely up to you. You can set goals according to the number of visitors, percentage increase in visitors, CPC, or some other benchmark.

After setting one or more measurable goals, make sure you have the analytics in place to track each ad's success. Facebook can provide you with some statistics that apply directly to your ad, such as number of impressions or number of times an ad was clicked. To measure click-through or conversion rates, however, you must have analytics installed on your website or landing page. Google Analytics (google.com/analytics) is an excellent choice, and it's free!

The goal you set influences your strategy and the type of advertising you choose to do on Facebook:

- **Pay-per-click advertising:** When you're paying per click, targeting ads to the most appropriate demographic and geographical area is of prime importance. In addition, make sure your ad and landing page (a Facebook page or a page on your website) are well coordinated to encourage and facilitate your call to action.

- **Pay-per-view advertising:** When you're paying for impressions, brand identity is most important. The graphic you use should clearly communicate your brand or company, and the text should be clear and informative.

Targeting a Demographic and Locale

Make the most of the targeting features in Facebook ads. If you're running a local pizzeria, advertising to the entire country is probably a bad idea—especially if you're offering free delivery. You'll get more bang for your advertising buck by targeting a specific location. Likewise, if whatever you're advertising is more likely to appeal to a certain age group or gender, specify your target demographic when creating your ad.

Listing a Few Keywords

For search engine optimization (SEO), web marketers work with their webmasters to insert code in the form of Meta data for a web page's title, description, and keywords to attract search-engine attention and improve page rankings in search results. Keywords, as it turns out, play a similar role in Facebook ads—enabling you to precisely target ads to Facebook users who express an interest in a certain topic (by mentioning it in their Profiles, Wall or Timeline posts, notes, and even in their status updates).

Precise interest targeting, as Facebook calls it, lets you define your ideal audience by what they're interested in, using terms people have shared in their Facebook profiles via their interests, activities, education, and job titles; Facebook pages they like; or the groups they frequent.

Prior to creating an ad, invest some thought in which words and phrases Facebook members are likely to use in describing themselves and their interests.

Settling on a Call to Action

Every ad, especially the pay-per-click variety, should include a call to action—a clear, direct message telling whoever is looking at the ad what to do. You usually want people to do two things: first, click on your ad, and then do something when they reach your Timeline or website or landing page, such as Like, register, order, shop, buy, obtain a quote, or check out special offers. These two goals should be well coordinated; if your ad sets certain expectations, your website or landing page must meet or exceed those expectations and facilitate the visitor's ability to follow through on your call to action.

A call to action may also apply to activity within Facebook, such as Liking a page, joining a brand-based group, or registering for an event.

Composing an Effective Message

In a Facebook ad, you don't have a lot of room to elaborate. You pretty much have to make your point in 25 words or fewer (25 characters for the title and 90 characters for the body). Use these words efficiently by composing a concise message that speaks clearly and directly to your audience. Here are some tips for creating quality ad copy:

- Be direct.
- Be clear.
- Keep it simple. Save the details for your website or landing page.
- Focus on the call to action.

- To reinforce brand identity, use your company or product name in the ad title or the body of the ad.

- Proofread the ad carefully before posting it. Nothing drives customers away more quickly than poor grammar and typos.

Finding Just the Right Picture

A high-quality image can catch the eye and reinforce the message your ad conveys. When selecting an image, make sure it's attractive and relevant to the product or service you're advertising.

The maximum image size is 80 pixels tall by 110 pixels wide, which is pretty small. If your image contains text, don't expect it to be readable. The image should have an aspect ratio (height:width) of 4:3 or 16:9. Facebook resizes the image for you, if necessary, but for best quality, size it yourself before uploading it. No animated graphics or flash images are allowed.

Prior to posting a photo or image, open it in a photo-editing or graphics program and play around with the brightness, contrast, and color balance to achieve the highest quality possible. Photos in particular often appear too dark when displayed on a computer screen. (For more about image quality, see Chapter 7.)

Launching Your Advertising Campaign

After laying the groundwork, launching your ad campaign is a snap. All you need to do is transfer your text, upload an image, specify your targeted demographic, and choose a plan and pricing. The following sections step you through the process.

Creating Your Ad

To get started, scroll to the bottom of any Facebook page, click **Advertising**, and click **Create an Ad** (upper-right corner). The

Create an Ad or Sponsored Story screen appears, where you enter information according to the onscreen prompts. As you enter information and preferences for your ad, Facebook prompts you to enter additional information and preferences that vary according to what you've entered so far. Question marks appear next to less-intuitive options; click a question mark to view additional information about the option.

With dozens of different ad configurations available to choose from—all of which Facebook does a great job of walking you through with simple prompts—you still might need a little help making sense of it all. The following list highlights key options/ stages in the ad-creation process and offers some guidance for each of them:

- **Destination:** Facebook enables you to link your ad to an external web page like a business website, or to content you've created on Facebook, like a Business page, event, or Facebook app.

- **What do you want to promote?** It's probably already occurred to you that if you promote a Facebook page, event, or app, more people can find, Like, or attend what you're promoting. But what if you could promote what a trustworthy person has said about your business, brand, or organization on Facebook, complete with that person's name and a link to her Facebook Profile? By choosing to promote a specific post that's on your page, you can do exactly that. Called a Sponsored Story, this ad format has been shown to have a higher click-through rate (CTR) and a lower cost per click than traditional Facebook ads. The format has become increasingly popular because it taps into how people already use Facebook. By highlighting News Feed stories that your fans have published about your business or brand, you appeal to members who choose to place their trust first and foremost in the word-of-mouth recommendations of people they know and trust.

- **People will see:** Depending on the destination you choose and what you specifically want to promote, Facebook provides you with options for what people will see when they view your ad. If you choose an external URL as the destination, for example, you're prompted to enter a headline and some text and upload an image. If you choose to promote a page or place (physical location), you can choose to have people see an ad you create or stories that their friends have posted or that have been posted about their friends related to the page or place.

- **Choose Your Audience:** By default, Facebook targets your ad to a very broad demographic—Facebook members 18 years and older who live in the default location (for example, the United States). Facebook enables you to narrow your focus by location, age, gender, Likes and interests, education, workplace, relationships, connections, and so on. Simply enter your preferences. As you change settings, Facebook displays (on the right side of the screen) an estimate of the number of members that fit the targeted demographic.

- **Connections:** Facebook gives you the option of displaying your ad or sponsored story to anyone or only those members who have a specific type of connection to your business or organization. For instance, if you want your ad to be seen only by people who already Like your page, you can choose that option under **Connections**.

- **Objective:** In Facebook-speak, objectives are "the goals that you have for your ad or sponsored story." You can choose from among getting people to click on your ad or sponsored story, Like a page, or install an app. Based on what you choose, Facebook shows your ad just to the members most likely to do what you choose as your objective.

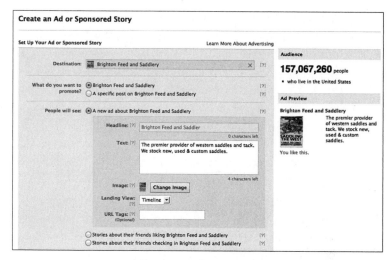

Create your Facebook ad.

Entering Campaign, Pricing, and Scheduling Preferences

After creating and targeting your ad, you must set up your ad campaign by entering your preferences for the following categories:

- **Campaign & Budget:** You can type a name for a new or existing campaign. Multiple ads in the same campaign share a daily budget and schedule. The budget is the total amount you want to spend per day or over the lifetime of the campaign.

- **Schedule:** You can choose to have your ad run continuously starting today or between two specified dates and times.

- **Pricing:** Here, Facebook shows you how you'll be charged for your ad. If your objective is to get people to click on your ad or sponsored story, you'll be charged per click (cost per click or CPC). If your objective is to get people to Like your page, you'll be charged per impression (cost per impression or CPM).

After entering your preferences, click the **Review Ad** button.

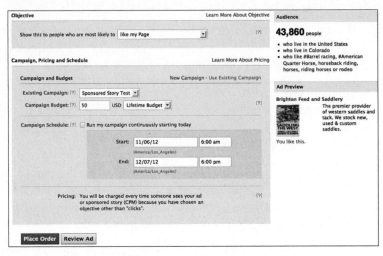

Enter campaign budget and scheduling preferences.

Reviewing and Approving Your Ad

The Review Ad page shows you how your ad will appear in Facebook, provides details about the ad campaign, and prompts you to enter payment information. Carefully examine your ad and all details about it. You can make changes by clicking the **Edit Ad** link. If you're happy with the ad, click **Place Order**.

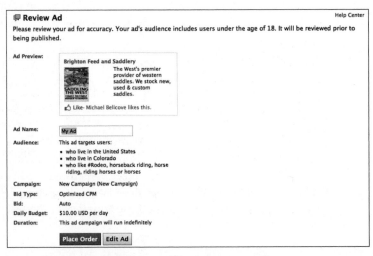

Review your ad and place your order.

Monitoring and Fine-Tuning Your Campaign

Your ad campaign is up and running. Now you can kick back, cross your fingers, and hope it meets your goals, right? Not quite. You should keep tabs on your campaign and be prepared to make adjustments.

After a day or two, check your ad's click-through rate, along with its total clicks, impressions, and average CPC or CPM. To view these statistics, click **Advertising** (at the bottom of any Facebook page) and then the name of the campaign on the following screen. From this page, you can click ad attributes to change them.

If your ad is not quite meeting your expectations, consider making any of the following adjustments:

- Try a different call to action if Facebook members are not responding to your ad.
- Adjust your targeting preferences to be more restrictive if your conversion rate is low, meaning that your ad is getting plenty of impressions or clicks but they aren't translating into the desired activity.
- Adjust your targeting preferences to be less restrictive if your ad's impressions or clicks are too low.
- Try simplifying your ad.
- Try a different image.

The Least You Need to Know

- Use ads as a component of your relationship-marketing efforts on Facebook. Don't expect them to generate direct sales.
- Prior to creating an ad, set a clear goal so you can measure its success.
- Prepare your ad copy and image prior to creating an ad, so you're not just slapping something together at the last minute.

- To create an ad, click **Advertising** (at the bottom of any Facebook page), click **Create an Ad**, and follow the on-screen instructions.

- You can monitor and make changes to ads at any time. Click **Advertising** and then click the name of the campaign on the following screen.

Glossary

account settings   Options that enable you to change your username, email address, and networks; make your account more secure; configure your notification settings; allow non-friends to subscribe to your posts; adjust settings for the apps and games you use; and more.

activity log   A complete and private record of what you're sharing on Facebook that enables you to remove or hide updates and other activities.

admin   Short for *administrator*, a Facebook member who has greater access and authority to manage and configure a group, page, or other user-generated area on Facebook.

app   Short for *application*, a Facebook plugin that adds functionality to Facebook, such as enabling users to upload photos or videos and play games.

badge   A clickable Facebook logo, such as "Find Us On Facebook," that you can add to your website or blog to connect it to your Facebook account.

block   A Facebook feature that enables you to prevent someone from accessing your Timeline or Profile, posting to your News Feed, or sending you messages or invitations.

Chat   A Facebook tool that enables friends to exchange text messages in real time.

comment   A remark posted in response to an existing status update or other content, such as a note, photo, or video.

cover   The area at the top of your Timeline, where you can post a picture that captures the essence of who you are.

Event   A Facebook app that enables you to announce special occasions or gatherings, invite Facebook users to attend, and keep everyone you invited posted about any developments related to the happening.

Facebook   An online social network that enables friends, family members, colleagues, classmates, acquaintances, businesses, brands, and organizations to get in touch and stay in touch and meet others who may share their interests or experiences.

fan   A term used to describe someone who "Likes" a Facebook page.

feed   A connection that pulls content from another source on the internet and displays it on Facebook.

footer   The area at the bottom of every Facebook page containing links to About Facebook, Advertising, Create a page, Careers, Terms, Help, and other offerings.

friend list   A subset of friends that provides you with an easier way to follow and communicate exclusively with that set of friends. Think of it as a clique.

friend request   A standardized message sent to another Facebook member whom you want to friend on Facebook.

friends   Any two people who mutually agree to connect with one another on Facebook.

friendship page   An area that contains the public Timeline or Wall posts and comments between two friends, photos in which they're both tagged, events they've both RSVP'd, and more. You can view a friendship page if you're friends with at least one of the members and have permission to view both members' Profiles.

Gift   A Facebook app that enables friends to exchange digital presents, which can sometimes be exchanged for real presents outside of Facebook.

Group   An area on Facebook where users with shared interests can gather. Groups can be exclusive or open to all.

Insights   A tool that provides developers and businesses with metrics regarding their content and the Facebook members who interact with it. Insights provide valuable data for analysis of user growth, demographics, and user-content interaction.

instant personalization   An optional feature that enables websites that have partnered with Facebook to personalize the content you see on their websites based on information gathered from your Facebook account.

left menu   The menu bar that runs along the left side of most Facebook pages and enables you to access the most frequently used Facebook features.

Like   A link you can click to indicate positive sentiment for something one of your friends or some other Facebook member has posted.

link   Text that a user can click to access the website it points to. Facebook enables members to share links via status updates.

member   Anyone with a Facebook account.

Messages   A Facebook feature that enables members to communicate with one another more privately. Messages between friends include actual messages, Facebook chatting, and any Facebook email they exchange.

Mobile   A Facebook app that enables you to log in to your Facebook account and use Facebook from a cell phone or other portable communications device.

network   An offline community of people related by locale or experience, such as a town, school, or place of employment.

News Feed   One of the main areas on Facebook, which displays activities your friends have chosen to share with you.

Notes   A core Facebook app that enables you to post longer entries than you'd normally post in a status update and provides a way to feed your blog (if you have one) into your Facebook Profile.

notification   A message Facebook sends you and/or displays on the notification list to let you know when something of importance has occurred, such as someone commenting on your status update or the receipt of a message.

page   A Facebook feature that's typically used to promote a business, organization, product, or brand.

Photos   A core Facebook app that enables you to upload digital photographs to your account and create, manage, and share photo galleries.

Places   A Facebook feature that enables members to share where they are, connect with friends nearby, and find special deals based on their current location. Businesses use Places to offer discounts and other specials.

Poke   A Facebook feature that enables you to let a friend know, in real time, that you're thinking about him.

privacy settings   Options that give you control over who can access what you share on Facebook and the type of content various people, such as the public or friends, can access.

Profile   A collection of information a Facebook member enters about herself along with an optional photo.

Publisher   The tool for posting Facebook status updates to a Wall or the News Feed.

RSS feed   *See* feed.

SMS   Acronym for *Short Message Service*, a technology that enables the exchange of text messages using a cell phone or other mobile communications device. Through the magic of SMS, you can also post content to Facebook using a mobile phone.

status update   A microblogging tool on Facebook that enables members to post brief messages, typically to share observations, insights, and experiences.

subscribe   To choose to enable a Facebook member's status updates to appear in your News Feed. You can subscribe to a member's status updates whether or not the person is your Facebook friend, assuming the person allows you to do so.

tag   To label yourself or a friend in a photo, video, note, or other item posted on Facebook. When you tag someone else, Facebook sends the person a notification.

Ticker   A live feed that appears on the right side of the screen showing all of your Facebook friends' activities as they occur. Ticker appears only if you and your friends are very active on Facebook.

Timeline   An online scrapbook consisting of stories, photos, videos, and Facebook activities that chronicle your existence on and off Facebook. You and your friends can post to your Timeline, and you can post to theirs.

top menu   The blue bar at the top of every Facebook page that enables you to access the most frequently used areas on Facebook.

Video   A core Facebook app that enables users to upload and share video clips.

Wall   A quieter area on Facebook where you and your friends can post status updates, comments, photos, video clips, links, and more. While the News Feed displays all activity, the Wall filters out a lot of stuff to focus more on your recent activity and what you and your friends specifically post on one another's Walls. Facebook is in the process of phasing out the Wall and replacing it with the Timeline.

video calling   A Facebook feature that enables you to video conference with Facebook friends, assuming your computer or smartphone is equipped to do so.

Index

Symbols

A

F

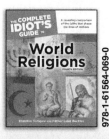